The CANNONBALL KID

DAVE HICKSON

deCoubertin
B O O K S

Published by deCoubertin Books Ltd in 2014.

deCoubertin Books, 145-157 St John Street, London, EC1V 4PY

www.decoubertin.co.uk

First hardback edition.

978-1-909245-07-5 – Standard edition

978-1-909245-20-4 – Special Edition

A CIP catalogue record for this book is available from the British Library.

Designed in Liverpool

Cover design by Leslie Priestley.

Limited Edition cover design by Steve Welsh.

Interior design by Thomas Regan at Milkyone Creative.

James Corbett would like to thank: George Gibson, Kate Highfield, Daniel Lewis, Leslie Priestly, Steve Welsh, Zoran Lucic, Paine Profitt, Thomas Regan, Harry and Philip Ross, Pat Labone, Bill Kenwright, Mark Rowan, Richard Kenyon, David France, Alan Myers, Neville and Emma Southall, Derek Mountfield, Howard Kendall, Bob Latchford, Dave Cockram, Wyn Williams, Don Roberts, Arthur Parker, Maria Parker, Steve and David Corley, Tony McNamara, John Sutherland, Jimmy Harris, Tom Gardner, Billy Butler, Claire Minter, Kevin Lewis, Mark Platt, Derek Temple, Gerry Moore, Billy Smith, Ivor Scholes, Derek Mayers, Alec Farrall, Ian Allen, Paul Cookson, Anna Corbett.

Printed and bound by Svet Print.

Photographs courtesy of Press Association, Getty Images, Colorsport, Mirrorpix and the author's collection.

Special thanks to Harry Ross for his support and friendship
to both Dave and Pat.

Foreword

BY BILL KENWRIGHT CBE

It has always been my belief that we have many idols throughout our lives – but only one hero.

Idols come in all shapes and sizes – at various times they can thrill us, teach us and inspire us. Heroes come in one size only. They are a Colossus. They thrill, teach and inspire at one and the same time. And then the truly great hero adds even more …

Growing up in Liverpool shortly after the war, we so needed a lift. A purpose, even. And maybe most of all a hero who would make us believe that the future could be ours.

I found all of those things in Dave Hickson. As a rather timid, quite often lonely lad, after making my journey to Goodison via a tram and two buses I felt totally at one with the world, totally safe, totally secure, when my hero ran out on to the pitch. He was Alan Ladd as Shane – but bigger! Errol Flynn as Robin Hood – but with a better quiff! Above all else he was my protector. If he was there for me I was safe! When I heard the frequent Goodison roar of 'Give it to Davy' I knew that my Everton family were at one with me. Almost alone he had an ability to make our hearts leap, our fears dissipate and our voices sing. We were Everton – and Everton had Dave Hickson.

It was no surprise to me that in 1954 a new comic strip was introduced to salute our hero! His fictional name was Roy Race, and he was Roy of the Rovers – but every Evertonian knew that the blond, almighty and unbeatable striker depicted in the Tiger every week was really our own Dave Hickson. I became an avid reader of the Tiger, and looked forward each week to seeing Dave's heroics in print as well as at the Blue and White Palace!

What made Dave Hickson one of the best-loved Everton players of them all? Was it simply because he followed the likes of Dixie the incomparable, and Tommy Lawton the majestic, and wore the number nine shirt – always the most revered at Everton? Was it because of the part he played in getting us back our First Division status after a brief time (very brief!) in the second tier? Was it because of his powerhouse, explosive style, putting his head in where others would fear to put even the boot? Or was it because of his most famous 90 minutes of all when with the referee pleading 'Take him off. The man's not normal!' and blood spurting out of a cut in his head, he scored the winning goal against Manchester United? It was all of those things – with one extra ingredient. We knew he was Blue. Through and through. As he famously said, 'I would have broken every bone

in my body for any of the clubs I played for – but I would have died for Everton.'

And we knew he meant it.

To me that summed up an Evertonian's love for his football club better than any words I could ever write. And funnily enough these words were *echoed* when, on the Liverpool–London train after only an average performance by the Blues, I witnessed John Motson commenting to an Evertonian that he must really love his club as he got up in the wee small hours every Saturday morning in Gillingham to support them. I promise you John's jaw physically dropped when the Bluenose in front of him looked John in the eye and said, quite simply, 'I would die for Everton.'

That is the loyalty that this football club endows on its supporters once they make the momentous decision to follow it – and we all know it will be a lifelong journey. Mine started with Dave Hickson. He has always been – and will always be – with me on my particular Everton journey. From the boys' pen, to the half-time gate, to the boardroom, to the chairman's seat. Without Dave I know, without even a glimmer of doubt, none of this would have happened. As a young Evertonian, he made me believe anything and everything was possible as long as you lead your team well – and most important of all, he instilled in me the courage to dare, and the belief that only by giving your all do you have the best chance of victory.

Finally, of many wonderful moments that Dave and I shared in his later life, my favourite was when I'd found his number (in the phone book!) in the mid-1980s, and rang him for the first time to see if he would join me and my family in our trek to Wembley where we were about to take on the Reds for the first time. With the humility that I soon learned was also a major part of the man's make-up, he accepted my invitation and travelled down with me and my lot to Wembley's twin towers. When the 30 or so of us got off the coach with the quiet, somewhat shy, still-blond maestro in our midst, we were soon engulfed by literally dozens and dozens of Evertonians. Shaking his hand, hugging him, thanking him, revering him! And, in some instances, thrusting their young kids in the air with cries of 'I named him after you, Dave' and most frequently 'Dave Hickson, you were my idol! And you still are.'

Visibly shaken, the Cannonball Kid, nearly three decades after he had worn the Everton Blue, broke down and wept. He truly had no personal idea of the legacy he had left behind – and ahead – of him. But why would he? Dave played at a time when there was little or no football on the television, and Saturday Sports Report was about the only time I remember hearing his name mentioned outside of Liverpool. But here he was at Wembley – in the 1980s and a Legend. A Colossus. A Hero.

You will read throughout the pages of this book the many magnificent exploits of Dave Hickson the footballer – and indeed the man. But more than anything, I hope that you will understand, even if only a little, just why he will always be the greatest of them all to me…

Thank you for the inspiration, my friend.

'Give it to Davy!!'

Bill Kenwright – Fan

Introduction

BY JAMES CORBETT

This story begins not with the Cannonball Kid, but another hero – mine.

Charles Mills, or Didi as he was known by my family, was my grandfather, my inspiration, my best friend. He was a great man and a great Evertonian; the finest I ever knew. He never played or worked for the club, nor really came into close contact with its playing staff or management. But for around 80 years he attended Goodison and bred a family of Evertonians. He witnessed every Everton number nine from Dixie Dean to James Beattie ('Beattie' was a word he would utter with a mixture of bemusement and horror late in his life) and the club, together with the Catholic Church and his family, was a central tenet of his life.

Every football-supporting family has its Charlie Mills somewhere in its sprawling tree. Football, I learned soon after falling in love with the game as a child in the mid-1980s, is not just about what happens on the pitch. It is about tradition, shared experience, community, history. My grandfather offered a link between an Everton past that went back to the club's virgin days in the nineteenth century when his own grandfather, an Irish immigrant from Tipperary, watched the first generation of royal blue heroes and my own son's generation in the twenty-first century, where footballers are global icons and multimillionaires.

Evenings at Didi's home in Crosby before a roaring fire, a glass of single malt to hand, would be spent recounting times gone by at Goodison. He attended his first game in April 1928, weeks before Dixie Dean plundered his historic 60th goal of the season. He witnessed some part of seven of Everton's nine league titles, was at three of their five FA Cup victories – the last with me, when he was aged 70, dancing down the steps of Wembley Stadium – and by my reckoning attended at least 1,500 Everton matches. He saw every Everton great, from Dean and Ted Sagar to Tim Cahill and Mikel Arteta. He saw and experienced so much, not just in football, but in life. But it wasn't at Wembley, or Goodison or Old Trafford or Villa Park, that he encountered some of his greatest moments as an Evertonian. It was high up on the windswept moors of East Lancashire.

Let me take you back. It is a spring night in Oldham. It is April 1953. Everton are not in a cup final, or on the brink of a league title, but ensconced in the Second Division, a dark place where they have resided for the past three seasons.

Fourteen years earlier it had been so different. Then they had won the league title with a team that included Tommy Lawton, Ted Sagar, Joe Mercer and the incomparable T.G. Jones, a man my grandfather claimed was the best player he saw in 80 years watching Everton. That team seemed set to dominate a generation. But three games into the 1939/40 season war had come and changed everything. For seven years there was no league football. My grandfather, aged 15 in 1939, came back – via Somaliland, Malaya, Egypt, Palestine and all places in between with the RAF – a man; his beloved champions returned as a diminished force.

Poor management imposed calamity on his fallen heroes. Mediocrity and then disaster followed. In the real world there was austerity, rationing, smog. The late 1940s and early 1950s were hard times in more ways than one. Then in 1951 Everton were relegated for only the second time in their history.

Just as everything seemed lost, so there came hope. Five games into life in the Second Division an outrageously brave centre forward was introduced from the reserves. With his distinctive quiff and the looks of a Boy's Own hero, he captivated Goodison with his swashbuckling play. He was fearless, at times playing like a human battering ram. He gave people belief where there was none. His name was Dave Hickson.

He was, recounted my grandfather in a brief memoir he wrote of his years as an Evertonian, 'inspiring, fearless – never a Dixie or a Lawton, but what a successor! The games he finished with his head covered with blood were numerous. It was just what the team needed – inspiration.'

Dave dragged a mediocre Everton team by the scruff of its neck and by April 1954 had pulled them back to the brink of where they belonged – the First Division.

Everton travelled to Oldham on the last day of the season needing a win to secure promotion. If they scored six goals they were Second Division Champions. My grandfather recalled:

In a hired charabanc with all my mates we arrived at the ground. The gates were shut and thousands were outside. The stewards were shouting, 'Sorry lads. The ground is overcrowded already.'

For the first 'and only' time we joined the mob. The gates crumbled and we all entered in one mad rush, just in time to see our first goal. Another three came before half-time. Mission accomplished.

The next 'plan' after the game was to find a pub. Late April, it was still light, but with about 55,000 Scousers well and hell bent with the same objective it seemed hopeless. Outside one pub, with about 100 trying for admission, the manager came out. 'No more in, lads, but I can fix you up in the back garden. Any trouble now and you're out.' We tipped our coach driver who, after our 'natural agreement', led us to the garden and kept his promise of drinking lemonade. That was until about 3am when he managed to get us out with the help of the proprietor.

It then dawned on me that 3am was the time that I started work – in Liverpool. Nemesis threatened.

I was put down in Queen Square (our then premises) to be met by my Dad – then my boss. His first words were 'You're late' (It was only 3.15am) and 'You've been drinking again.' (Is the Pope a Catholic?)

One of his fellow directors came to my aid: 'Come on Charlie – it's only a one off.'

'It had better be – otherwise he's out,' came the reply.

It had been, he recalled as he poured another whisky in his front room half a century later, 'probably one of the greatest nights of my life'.

To my grandfather Dixie Dean may have been incomparable, Tommy Lawton his hero, Roy Vernon and Alex Young eulogised. But Dave Hickson represented something different: he restored pride in hard times and offered hope when there was none. To a young man making his way in a difficult post-war world, it meant more than anything else.

Dave graced the Everton colours for 243 games, scoring 111 goals. He is sixth among Everton's all-time leading goalscorers. He never won anything, he never really came close to international recognition – a feat harder in an era of heroic centre forwards than it is today. He played for all three Merseyside clubs. He performed numerous heroic acts on the pitch. But the extraordinary thing about Dave Hickson was not really his feats on a football field, it was his effect on other people. People loved him, even those too young to see him play. He was idolised by a generation of fans. Everywhere he went, he was recognised, loved.

Speaking at his funeral Bill Kenwright recounted, 'I have a big photo of him in my office and I say, "That was the man who for a lot of kids like me – post-war kids in Liverpool, frightened, a bit shy, timid – looking for a hero, we found one in Dave Hickson."'

Even during his career, those watching him recognised that he was making history. His most famous game came on Valentine's Day 1953, when in an FA Cup fifth round tie in front of Goodison's second highest ever crowd, he returned to the field with a gaping head wound to score the winning goal for Second Division Everton against the League Champions, Manchester United.

On the following Monday the *Liverpool Echo* correspondent – foretelling my own experiences, and probably those of a generation of Evertonians – wrote in the style of a grandfather recounting a story:

Everton v Man United programme 1953

> **I never in all my life seen a player wi' so much guts as young Davie showed. Wi' the blood streaming down 'is face 'e got stuck into 'is job like as if 'is very life depended on it. Twice the referee suggested 'e should go off for attention but Dave waved 'im aside just like a teetotaller refusing a drink.**
>
> **Well, I'll grant 'em Liddell were a great player, but that day our Davie were as much a match-winner as Liddell at 'is best.**
>
> **That game against United is always called 'ickson's match.**

What was Dave like? It was difficult to reconcile the rabble-rouser and hard man of contemporary reports with the sweet old man that no one would say a bad word about. Even during his career, football reporters would reflect on this contradiction inherent in Hickson.

'For a quiet, self-effacing man like Hickson to cause such controversy among fans on Merseyside is one of the most inexplicable things about him,' were the prescient words of the *Liverpool Echo's* Michael Charters in 1959. 'Whatever Hickson did on the field he never went out from the dressing room other than determined to play the game and nothing but

the game, but his enthusiasm for the cause and the idolising effect of his many fans often made for trouble.'

Certainly he had a petulant side on the pitch that was out of keeping with his modest demeanour off it. Footage of Tranmere Rovers' 1963 FA Cup tie with Chelsea shows him like a proto-Duncan Ferguson or Luis Suárez, grappling and punching an opponent at one point, arguing with the referee at another and attracting the condemnation of the commentator. 'I just wanted to win,' Dave would say. 'I was just determined to do everything I could for my team.'

He felt victimised by referees, both during and after his career. In days when footballers were supposed to show deference to all in authority, particularly referees, there was a lingering stigma to his disciplinary record. One story has Hickson sat in a compartment of a train at Lime Street at the height of his fame when a guard's whistle blew. Dave popped his head out of the windows and enquired, 'What have I done now, ref?' Such was his sense of humour I can imagine the tale having some basis in fact.

He was approaching the end of his life in the period I spent most time with him, and I last saw him around a month before his death. I always found him funny, self-deprecating, generous. Everybody knew him. Everybody loved him. He was obsessed with football. He loved Everton. He loved the Everton chairman Bill Kenwright like a son, and considered his family as an

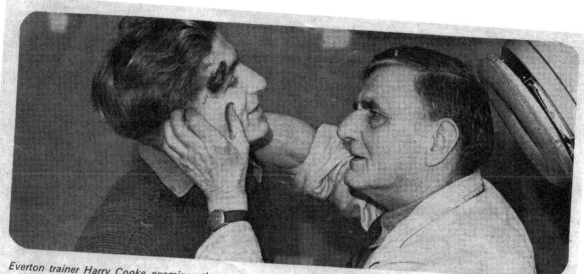

Everton trainer Harry Cooke examines the gaping wound that handicapped Dave Hickson in a famous Cup-tie.
Picture: Liverpool Echo

To many people the name Dave Hickson was spelled . . . G-U-T-S. And, if any one game ever earned a man a reputation, then that match was the Fifth Round F.A. Cup battle – and we do mean "battle" – between Second Division Everton and the Football League Champions, Manchester United, before a 70,000 Goodison Park crowd on February 14th 1953.

St. Valentine's Day? Dave must have had many a chuckle about that as he recalled surging through the second half to grab the winner despite a gaping wound over his right eye. Said *"Ranger"* of the *Liverpool Echo:* "Hickson gave a magnificent display of indomitable courage throughout the second half when blood was streaming from a cut over the eye."

A glance at the picture above will show you the damage that was done five minutes before half-time when Hickson, with a typically brave attempt, flung himself at a Lindsay cross and *"came into contact with an opponents boot."* Blood simply pumped from the gash and he was led off by trainer Harry Cooke with a wad of cotton wool held to his face.

But we're getting ahead of ourselves. Throughout, it was a strong, aggressive Cup-tie with Everton refusing to stand off and allow United to dictate the pace and pattern of the game. Hickson, however, had quickly served notice that he was going to give Chilton a trying afternoon.

Everton could have had a penalty when Byrne pulled Cummins down, but the referee ignored the appeals. In the 27th minute that fine winger Johnny Berry paved the way for Rowley to put United in front. As the *Echo* saw it:

"Berry was the man who should get most credit, though Rowley was the scorer. Berry, out on his own on the right, foxed Lindsay with a feint to centre. Instead, he turned inside, beat his man, and tried a shot which O'Neill dived to parry. The goalkeeper could not gather the ball, however, and the rebound went to Rowley who lashed it into the net from six yards."

Everton hit back immediately with Buckle going close with a shot and then a header. After 34 minutes, however, it was "Flash" Eglington who pulled Everton

level. Tommy was having a fine goal-scoring time at this point, for he had scored in the previous four matches.

This time Cummins fed Hickson on the right and he transferred it to Eglington, cutting in from the left. He waltzed round Aston and then – with his RIGHT foot if you don't mind – planted a great drive past Wood from ten yards.

So, at half time, with everyone speculating whether Hickson would re-appear for the second half, the scene was set for some of the most dramatic 45 minutes of football ever seen at Goodison. Re-appear? Hickson had hardly set foot on the field before he had thumped a header against an upright!

Needless to say, it didn't do his cut much good and after more treatment, the referee went across to see if Hickson wanted to go off. Hickson waved him away and ran upfield ready for more combat.

Blood was now streaming down Hickson's face, which had become a scarlet mask. Eglington lobbed just over; Buckle was up-ended and another penalty appeal refused; but in the 63rd minute, Hickson's courage was rewarded with an incredible solo goal.

It began when Clinton, on the half way line, clipped a ball upfield to Eglington, who smartly switched it inside to Hickson. Dave seemed to have no chance for two defenders were in close attendance. But, with the tenacity and persistence that hall-marked his game, he decided to take them on.

He chested the ball down, beat one man, side-stepped another and then screwed back an oblique shot which Wood failed to reach.

This goal put Everton well and truly on top and United in desperation moved Aston up to centre forward. But there was no loosening Everton's hold now. Indeed Hickson, one side of his face covered with blood, managed to lay on two chances for John Willie Parker before the whistle went and goalkeeper O'Neill ran half the length of the pitch to embrace the centre forward.

It was a display worthy of the Cup Final but Everton were destined to be K.O'd by Bolton in the Semi-Final. But that's another story . . . . .

21

A teenage Dave with the legendary Everton chairman, Will Cuff.

extension of his own. He took enormous pride in the ambassadorial role he had held with Everton for nearly two decades. Even though he was frail and not in the best of health, he was insistent that he would fulfil his match-day duties.

He dearly missed his second wife, Pat, who had passed away in November 2010. Following her death Everton filled an increasingly large personal void in his life. At times he would get very emotional about both of them. He lived his life from Everton match to Everton match, and would draw comparisons between the hard-working teams of David Moyes and those in which he had played himself. I asked him who in modern football he most resembled as a player and he replied, 'Victor Anichebe,' the oft-maligned journeyman forward who scored 18 times for Everton between 2005 and 2013. In a late-1990s interview with the author Becky Tallentire, he had answered 'Dion Dublin'.

Like the Moyes era, the Everton teams of the 1950s always fell just short. Dave was convinced 2013 was going to be the year Everton again lifted the FA Cup. Looking back now, it would

have been a fitting send-off for the Cannonball Kid, but they couldn't manage it. Dave was devastated by their quarter-final defeat to Wigan in March 2013.

We would usually meet in the Nags Head pub in the Cheshire village of Willaston across the road from his home. He would sup halves of Guinness and order off-menu, insisting that he was only served child-sized portions. 'Make sure they bring lots of ketchup,' he would say. 'I love ketchup!'

We would talk for two or three hours, always about football, but – despite being there under the premise of working on his autobiography – not just about him. He was rarely critical about a colleague or opponent. Although his memory was sometimes hazy, his knowledge of the game was huge. Sometimes he would come out with a detail or an incident that had happened 60 years previously. As a journalist it is your duty to be sceptical, to question, to check. Sometimes I couldn't believe things that I was hearing, but I would look it up later and invariably Dave would be right about a long-forgotten moment or incident or player.

At the same time he had an official history of himself – centred around the 1953 FA Cup run, promotion the following year, and his status as a number nine icon – that he liked to recount and refer to. He joked about his still magnificent blond quiff, and would describe the technique of rubbing soap and Vaseline into his hair to hold it in place. Although 50 years older than me, he possessed around 50 times the amount of hair, so such information was largely lost on myself.

As his biographer, transcending this official version of his life was sometimes tricky. There were parts – such as his messy departure from Liverpool, after he fell out with Bill Shankly – that he wouldn't discuss, or would just gloss over. I sensed at times that he felt slightly ashamed of his poor disciplinary record, but he would never exactly say so. He probably came closest to the truth about this in a 1955 interview when he said he did not attempt to 'justify' his disciplinary record, 'but would like to say in partial extenuation that everything I have done has arisen solely out of my desire for the success and well-being of the club that has employed me'.

He came from an era before footballers' non-footballing lives were of public interest, and although he was always happy to talk about his second wife, Pat, he was insistent that the rest of his family were not discussed in this book to maintain their privacy.

His sense of humour could be wicked. With dark irony he would joke about completing the book 'before they carry me away in a box'. Sometimes he would make a play on being a befuddled old man when really he knew exactly what was going on. On one occasion he had been asked by a friend of a friend to obtain a large Everton flag that could be wrapped around the coffin of a young Evertonian who had recently passed away. The chairman of a nearby supporters club was summoned and they reviewed a selection of Everton banners for the task. These had been made up for away games, and were large enough for a coffin – larger than those available in the club shop, anyway – but many boasted completely inappropriate slogans.

'What about that one?' said Dave, innocently pointing to a flag emblazoned with 'Kopites are Gobshites'.

'I don't think the Reverend would like that, Dave.'

'Suppose not,' he said. 'What about that one?'

There was an impish glint in his eye as he pointed at a banner bearing the Everton crest and the legend 'We will never have your shame'.

'Dave, the last thing this poor lad's family are going to see are the words "We will never have your shame" as he's lowered into the ground.'

'Suppose so,' he said, a roguish grin betraying the fact that he was merely winding us all up.

The Everton flag he eventually settled upon bore the dictum of his old teammate and friend Brian Labone: 'One Evertonian is worth twenty Liverpudlians'. Whether, as a former Liverpool player, he consciously believed that motto is another matter. Dave was always very respectful towards his former club, something that was reciprocated by the Red fraternity.

Dave in action for (top) Tranmere Rovers and (bottom) Liverpool.

What is clear is that from the moment he first pulled on a red shirt in 1959, many Liverpool fans not only dismissed their concerns about signing an Everton icon, but seemed entirely enraptured by him. On his debut against Aston Villa, 11,000 more spectators turned up to see Liverpool that day than had done so in the league all season, although many had also crossed from Goodison to see their idol. As the *Liverpool Echo* correspondent noted, 'One rabid Liverpudlian, disgusted at having two Anfield doors closed in his face on Saturday, told me; "It's coming to something when a Liverpudlian can't get into Anfield for so-and-so Evertonians …"'

At the time Hickson described his Liverpool debut as 'one of the most wonderful days of my life'. He scored twice that day and was hailed as the 'Red Dean', sentiments that were probably enhanced by his magnificent scoring record during the remainder of the 1959/60 season: 21 goals from 27 appearances, the most prolific spell of his career. In so doing he became one of the very few to transcend the great Mersey football divide.

His career at Anfield ended disappointingly in May 1961. Bill Shankly and Dave Hickson, red and blue icons, was never a match made in heaven. They were too strong willed, too stubborn, too unyielding. Twice Shankly had managed him and twice Hickson had not been his signing. At Huddersfield in 1957, Dave was desperate for a move back to Goodison and the parsimonious Everton board, knowing this, had consciously squeezed every last penny they could from the Terriers' asking price. Shankly would not have been impressed by this humiliation.

In 1961 Liverpool had narrowly missed out on promotion to the top flight, the poor run of form that cost them promotion coinciding with a period in which Dave had been dropped by his manager. Despite asking for a transfer, he returned to the team as the season petered out to its disappointing conclusion. Liverpool wanted £10,000 for him, a fee beyond most clubs in the lower leagues – the stage where Dave was now expected to play – and so the Cannonball Kid announced he was quitting football, to go into business with Liverpool's young winger Kevin Lewis. It seems as if the announcement was somehow a ruse to secure Hickson a free transfer (Lewis told me while I was writing this book that he had no idea how his name was brought into the dispute) with Dave immediately signing for Cambridge City.

Dave did not speak of this, but he would recall with pride his return to Merseyside and league football with Tranmere Rovers via Bury in 1962. In so doing he became only the second player, after the 1920s goalkeeper Frank Mitchell, to play for all three Merseyside clubs. (A third, John Heydon, did not make a senior Everton appearance, while Kevin Sheedy played for Everton and Liverpool and coached Tranmere.) He enjoyed a decent 18 months at Prenton Park,

before embarking on a brief managerial adventure with Ballymena and Ellesmere Port Town.

In the mid-1960s he entered civilian life, working as a rat catcher for Ellesmere Port Council. He still considered himself a footballer, even as an old man. I once asked him how he old he was when he finally stopped playing, meaning as a professional. 'Seventy-seven,' he replied, without missing a beat, 'and that was only because I had my heart attack.' Even after last pulling on his boots, he lived every game in his head.

His team, 'The Over the Hill Mob', were well known for partaking in charity matches across Merseyside, and it was as a veteran that he finally played at Wembley, turning out in pre-match encounters before Everton's run of 1980s FA Cup finals. During the summer he played tennis and cricket until in his seventies.

Although he lived his life through football, like a lot of old players in civvie street, he said he did not venture back to Goodison very often. That changed in 1994 when he retired from his job on the council and two days later took a call from Bill Kenwright with the offer of an ambassadorial job at Everton. 'How would you like to come back, son?' were the words that Dave recounted again and again, with pride and wonder.

Thus began the final chapter of his life, as an official icon; a living, breathing part of Everton history, who prowled the corridors and anterooms of Goodison day in, day out for the rest of his days. With Pat he worked energetically for charities, notably the Lily Centre and the Everton Former Players Foundation, who – in accordance with Dave's wishes – will receive the royalties from this book. In 2011 his contribution to these causes saw him made a Citizen of Honour of the City of Liverpool.

So often old heroes are shunted aside, forgotten about or, worse, exploited. Not Dave. Everton treated him like the legend that he was and he repaid that with the same commitment he had shown while a player during the 1950s. Everybody connected with the club recognised that. Everybody knew him, everybody loved him.

My reasons for collaborating with Dave on this book are personal, slightly sentimental even. They're born not from my grandfather's memories of him, nor any great desire to write another Everton book. Instead it started with an encounter between my grandfather and Dave in late 2006. Aged 82, Didi was stooped and increasingly frail by then, a little forgetful at times. He had given up on going to Goodison – though never on Everton – a year earlier, when

Top: Dave with his great friend Brian Labone.

Bottom: Meeting his co-author's late grandfather, Charles 'Didi' Mills, in 2006, an encounter that belatedly resulted in publication of this book.

Hickson, pictured in December 1963, in the bookmakers he ran on Scotland Road during the 1960s.

the club moved his season ticket reserved seat to make way for corporate seating. He was finding the crowds a struggle by that stage and the spectre of another flight of stairs to watch James Beattie was too much.

Losing that part of his routine left a great void in his life that we tried to fill in other ways. One December morning I and two of my brothers took him to Goodison Park for a behind-the-scenes tour. We were the only visitors that sunny winter's day. Our host? Bequiffed, immaculate, endearing – you've guessed it.

For two hours, far more than our allotted time, Dave showed us every nook and corner of the Old Lady. He was patient and kind with my grandfather, helping him on the stairs. Afterwards we sat and drank coffee with him and he listened patiently to the recollections of an old man. We talked about that day for months afterwards. It made our year.

I like to think that Dave saw that my grandfather was a little lost, that he needed a hero's touch, but I probably realise now he was a little like that with everybody.

I saw Dave every now and then after that day, and always thanked him for his time. We discussed doing a book on one occasion, but it came to nothing.

Then in October 2012, I was with him at a dinner at Goodison Park. Dave was nearly 82 by then, the same age as my grandfather when he was shown around Goodison. Dave was increasingly frail and Pat had passed away a couple of years earlier. My grandfather had also died two months before. I too was a little lost without him.

'How's about we do that book?' he asked.

I'm so very glad that he asked. His subsequent company and friendship over the last months of his own life helped me through a difficult period and eased my own sadness. I was born 40 years too late to ever see him play, but I too finally got the chance to revel in the aura of a football great.

What follows is not a conventional autobiography. Work on it was seven months down the line when Dave passed away in July 2013. Many of the interviews needed to complete an autobiography had been finished, but some of the finer details, the verification, the approval for aspects of his story, were still to be undertaken. I have had to leave some parts out because some questions were carried to the grave unanswered. At times I take up the story and fill in gaps. My contributions, supplemented

at times by the great cache of letters and
documents that Dave kept, are italicised.

What made Dave such a unique and fascinating
figure was not just the heroics he performed on
the pitch, but the humility and small acts of
kindness he showed off it. He had a huge effect
upon very many people. People like my
grandfather, people like Bill Kenwright;
Evertonians, Liverpudlians, kids from Ellesmere
Port. Their stories and their responses to the
Cannonball Kid are worthy of inclusion because
they bring context to his story and colour some
of the blanks in the life of a Merseyside football
legend. I hope I've done Dave proud, as he did
all of us.

James Corbett, Liverpool and Ireland.

December 2013.

*Dave with his friend
Dixie Dean in the 1970s.
Dixie had coached Dave
as a young player three
decades earlier.*

The Cannonball Kid

DAVE HICKSON

'Everton is my football life. When I go out into the middle I do not play for directors, managers, spectators or myself. I play for Everton. The only thing that worries me in this business is the feeling that somewhere, somehow, I am not wanted any longer at Goodison Park.'

Dave Hickson, September 1959

The final week of October 1929 was a tumultuous one in world affairs. This had nothing to do with Dave Hickson's entry into the world in Salford on Wednesday 30th (although some of the defenders he came up against years later may have disagreed!) but because the New York Stock Exchange had lost some $30billion in value earlier that week. I suppose you could say it was the first bit of bad timing on Dave's part; although the market rallied on the day he was born, the stage was set for a period of unparalleled financial depression, which would be felt globally. As people throughout Europe were left with nothing there was a lurch to the political extremes, which, a decade later, resulted in war.

Those interwar years were a period of struggle for many people. Work was scarce and at times hard to come by. My parents, Harry and Alice, were part of a generation that moved in order to find work and when I was six months old they made a journey of around 40 miles to Ellesmere Port in Cheshire to take up work at the Bowater Paper Mill. For most of the rest of my life I would call this area home.

Bowater's was one of the area's main employers and at its peak would employ 1,500 people, providing around 60 per cent of Britain's newsprint. My dad worked there in charge of the ink stores, my mum worked there and on leaving school I also worked there.

We lived in a small house on Rossmore Road; just me, my mum and dad, and my younger brother Peter, who was born a couple of years after me. It was a happy childhood, stable, and although we never had much, we never wanted for anything either. My parents were strait-laced, really straightforward people, but beneath those outward impressions my dad was a very witty man.

Despite growing up in the Great Depression, an era of mass unemployment and hunger marches, I was really sheltered from the unfolding turmoil. Perhaps I was lucky because my parents had steady jobs at the paper mill. Or maybe it's because I had football running through my veins. It was my obsession, my love, my reason for being, and would remain so for the rest of my life.

My first memories of football are of kicking a ball on the way to school, aged about six or seven. After that there was no escape. It was football, football, football. We played at school, we played after school, we played on the weekends and through the holidays. We played in the morning and until the last bit of sun had left the sky.

Although I became synonymous with Everton and achieved renown as the only senior footballer to play for all three Merseyside clubs, my allegiance initially lay in the city of my birth. Manchester United were my team and I was very keen on them throughout my childhood. We were back and forth to Salford all the time and my interest in United was heightened by a couple of trips to Old Trafford on visits there. Being part of that magnificent throng of people cheering on our heroes was something else, something I thought was without comparison – until I actually played in front of those same people. That was even better!

United, during the 1930s, were going through a barren patch, however, and spent most of the decade yo-yoing between the First and Second Divisions. I suppose it was my bad timing again.

My adopted town of Ellesmere Port had a great football heritage and growing up we were all aware of the outstanding players from the Port that had made the step up to the professional game. Sam Chedgzoy was a dazzling outside right who starred for Everton and England on either side of the First World War, and at Goodison his wing play nurtured a fellow Wirralian, Dixie Dean, in the early years of his career. Joe Mercer, an Everton and England wing half, was one of the finest players of the 1930s. His own father, Joe senior, had also served as a professional with Nottingham Forest and Tranmere, and previously played as an amateur for Ellesmere Port Steelworks with Chedgzoy. Then there was Stan Cullis, a dazzling defender for Wolves and England, who became one of the most highly rated managers in the post-war era.

I attended Joe Mercer's old primary school at John Street. I was never really academically minded, I was just focused on sport. Although we knew great footballers came from the Port, and despite my visits to Old Trafford, I wasn't really conscious of professional football while growing up. It was a very different world back then. Now I can turn on Sky and watch football virtually every second of the day. There's pages and pages of coverage in the newspapers every single day. There's mobile phones, magazines, loads of books – it's brilliant! Back then there was none of that technology. It's true that there were comics and magazines and cigarette cards, but the sort of immersion in the professional game you have now simply wasn't prevalent. Or rather, it wasn't part of my life growing up. Instead of worshipping other players, I merely focused on my own game.

In September 1939, after years of heightening tensions through Europe, war finally broke out. As with my experience of the Great Depression, I was one of the lucky ones. Dad was never sent to fight. Liverpool was heavily blitzed, but in Ellesmere Port – despite there being lots of factories nearby – we were really on the edge of it all. We had an air-raid shelter at the bottom of our garden, a basic Anderson shelter dug into the ground, and we used to go there every night. It was a bit of an adventure at first, and sometimes frightening, but we went so often that we didn't really think about it too much in the end.

I think sometimes when you're a child you tend to overlook important things that are going on in the world. We were conscious of the war, of course we were, and we were affected by things like rationing. You really couldn't buy anything without a ration book. But besides that, and the nights spent in the air-raid shelter after the roar of the sirens, it didn't affect me really. It's only now, many, many years later, that I look back and see what we all went through – what happened and what could have happened – and think how wonderful it was the way that everybody coped with it all.

Howard Kendall

FORMER PLAYER AND MANAGER OF EVERTON FOOTBALL CLUB

Howard Kendall is Everton's most successful manager as well as one of the club's greatest players. He got to know Dave during his retirement.

As an Everton player – at least in my day in the 1960s and 1970s – you weren't always very aware of who'd preceded you in a blue shirt. I suppose it was before the days when old players were really welcomed back to the club on match day and I'm very glad that's changed now. Unlike the old days, whenever you go to Goodison now you see all the old players, invited as guests of the chairman or the club.

That's really how I got to know Dave Hickson. From the mid-1990s onwards, always waiting at the entrance was Dave. He was always so welcoming, so happy to see you. It was the first thing that you'd see when approaching the ground, and you'd think, 'Ah, it's Dave.' Really, it should have been Dave that was welcomed by everyone else, but he wouldn't have it any other way.

He loved the club and loved being a part of it, even when he was an old man. I think it's lovely, absolutely fabulous, the way that he was a part of the club until the very end.

Dave's school reports in this era show a hard working, above average student. His end of year report in July 1943, when he was aged 13, record 'Very Good' for arithmetic, literature and science. 'High standard has been kept throughout the year. Marks show general ability,' wrote his teacher. Dave finished the year marked twelfth out of 44 students.

One advantage of living through the war as a boy and then a teenager was the opportunities it afforded me. Because so many men were away fighting and industrial demand was high, there was never any shortage of work. I left school aged 14 in 1944 and walked straight into a job at the paper mill, same as my parents. I worked in Bowater's laboratory until I was called up for national service at the age of 18.

The shortage of manpower also benefited my football career. The endless hours kicking tennis balls around the back streets of Ellesmere Port and playing in schoolboy and park games had paid off. I had also grown a lot since becoming a teenager. I was a strong, powerful centre forward; scoring goals was my passion. Crucially, I could look after myself. So when Ellesmere Port Town signed me shortly after I left school, I knew I was ready – even at the age of 14.

The club had been founded in 1924 as Ellesmere Port FC and twice finished bottom of the Cheshire County League before folding and being re-formed as Ellesmere Port Town. They were a good amateur club, well supported, and would in 1948 rejoin the Cheshire County League from the Liverpool County Combination League after a gap of two decades. There were some good players, like Tommy Lewis – whose son Kevin would go on to play alongside me for Liverpool – and Eric Purcell, a fine left winger. They also possessed – when he was in the mood for a game – one of the finest centre forwards of the interwar years in Tom 'Pongo' Waring.

Pongo had been Dixie Dean's successor as Tranmere Rovers' centre forward in the mid-1920s and his goalscoring feats, while not the equal of Dean, were not far off. A double hat-trick for Tranmere against Durham City preceded a big-money move to Birmingham, where he established himself as a Villa legend. In 226 appearances for Villa he scored 167 goals, including 10 hat-tricks, and a club record 49 league goals in the 1930/31 season. Twice in this era Villa finished First Division runners-up. He even kept Dean out of the England team, scoring four goals in five international appearances.

In the veteran stage of his career and as wartime football usurped the league programme, he turned out for a number of Wirral and Cheshire clubs, including Ellesmere Port Town. It was my job, fresh out of school, to partner him in the Town attack. It was quite an undertaking, but nothing ever fazed me, not even Pongo's extrovert character.

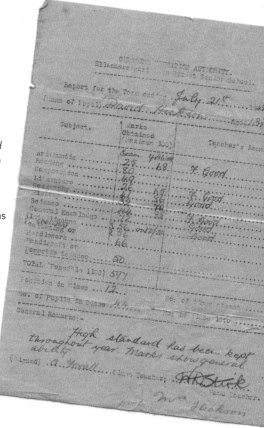

Dave's reports from John Street School showed an above average student

As a kid, I was fairly oblivious to this, but Pongo had a reputation throughout football as a bit of a strange character. In his autobiography, *Soccer in the Blood*, the Villa captain Billy Walker wrote of him:

There were no rules for Pongo. Nobody knew what time he would turn up for training – ten o'clock, eleven o'clock, twelve o'clock, it made no odds. Nobody on the staff could do anything with him although I think I can claim, as the captain in his days, to be the only person able to handle him. He was a funny lad indeed. We started the week's training on Tuesday mornings and every Tuesday he followed a habit which he could never break. He would go round all the refreshment bars on the ground and finish off the lemonade customers, storing the remains in the bottles! Then he would start a little of his training – but that seldom lasted very long.

Looking back it was a great honour to play at such a young age with an England international but, like a lot of things, I never really thought too much about it at the time. I was just interested in playing as much as my work hours at Bowater's would permit. Getting paid expenses for doing what I loved at Ellesmere Port Town was just an unexpected bonus, although we never got anything more than that.

My performances during the war years soon started to attract the attention of Merseyside's professional clubs. Both Liverpool and Everton came down to see me and I suppose Tranmere must have done as well. Everton had a scout in the Ellesmere Port area called Tom Corley and he recommended me for a trial at Goodison.

Of course, I was incredibly excited at the opportunity, but I didn't really have any notion of what being a professional footballer entailed or that I could make a living from the game. In fact that wasn't even on the agenda at the time. Like most First Division clubs, Everton had a huge array of players representing them, the majority as amateurs. As well as the first team and the reserves, which were filled with professionals, there was an A Team, a B Team and, back then, even a C Team.

The ranks of these junior teams were filled mostly with hopeful kids, like me. You couldn't sign as a professional until you were 18 in any case. The chances of ever making the grade were very slim, but by affiliating themselves with the best amateur and youth players, it enabled clubs like Everton to keep a hold of you should you be one of the lucky few to look like stepping up.

To be honest, I just wanted to play. Whether that was with my friends in the park, for Ellesmere Port Town or Everton, didn't really concern me too much at that age. Although they were reigning League Champions through the war years and the likes of Dixie Dean and Tommy Lawton were immortal names, I'd never even seen Everton play.

I took the tram, ferry and bus to Goodison – a journey I would repeat many times over the years, though not – as I did in 1944 – with a gas mask on my back. My carefree attitude soon changed the first time I saw Goodison's magnificent structure. It was super. I was in awe. I wanted to play there. As if in a dream, Joe Mercer greeted me along with T.G. Jones, the great Welsh international centre half. I was a nobody, a strapping teenage hopeful, just one of many with a slim chance of making it. But they took the time to welcome me, make me feel at home, as if I were a contender. It's something I've never forgotten.

'All the best in your career,' said Joe, as I left them.

I was determined then that I was going to make it.

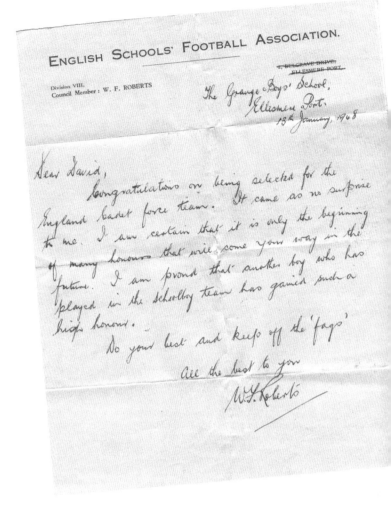

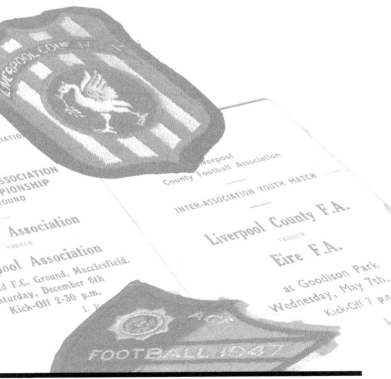

Tom Corley
THE MAN WHO DISCOVERED LEGENDS

It is fair to say that Tom Corley, the man who 'discovered' Dave Hickson for Everton, led a life less ordinary.

Born in Chester in 1881, he played football as a goalkeeper to a high standard in Sheffield – and was possibly at one stage on the books of Sheffield Wednesday – before a broken leg ended his hopes of a top-class career. He subsequently served as a PT instructor for the British Army during the First World War and as part of the expeditionary force in Russia during the subsequent Bolshevik War.

A friend of the great Everton winger Sam Chedgzoy, his connection with the Blues solidified when he ran the Mersey Ironworks Club, a social club popular with Everton players in the interwar years. 'My dad actually worked behind the bar and I remember him telling me that Dixie Dean used to come in,' recalls Tom's grandson, David Corley. 'If Everton had won he'd put his hand in his pocket and pull out a big load of half-crowns, thrown them on the bar and the drinks would be on him.' Around this time he began scouting for Everton.

Tom Corley's first great contribution to the Everton cause came when he spotted Joe Mercer in the 1920s and introduced him to the club. They became close family friends and Mercer was best man at Corley's daughter's wedding. He discovered other players, notably Stan Cullis, the great Wolves' half back.

'He'd become a really notable figure in Ellesmere Port from a sports point of view,' says David Corley. 'And this is not myth; this is something I've actually seen for myself. He organised Cup Final trips, I think probably two or three coachloads. Not when Everton were there necessarily, but for every Cup Final. He'd organise the meals, he'd organise accommodation if that was appropriate, all the coaches and so on. So he became a sort of Mr Football in the area.'

In the 1940s, Tom became manager of Bowater Sports and Social Club, attached to the large print factory where Hickson's parents worked and Dave would himself find employment when he left school. It was Tom that recommended Dave to Everton (not Dixie Dean as some accounts have erroneously pointed out) during the war years, and they kept in contact until well into Dave's playing days. When Dave made his first-team debut in 1951, among the many telegrams was one signed 'Dad, Mam, Peter [Hickson's brother] and also Mr Cawley [sic]'.

Now an old man, Tom continued to be what his grandson describes as 'an avid football fan'. George Sharples, the wing half who made 10 Everton appearances in the early 1960s and played for Blackburn and Southport, was one of his later finds. He too was from Ellesmere Port. 'Kids of my school were being scouted by him as well; so we are talking there about the very late 50s, possibly even 1960, that he was still active as a scout,' says David.

Tom Corley died in April 1961. He was, recalled the *Ellesmere Port Pioneer*, 'An outstanding personality in local football circles and a man who discovered several players who achieved stardom.'

We played a trial match at Bellefield and I played one half at the back and one half up front. I don't remember much about it, but for the fact that we won 7–1 and I scored one of the goals, diving through a big puddle of water to score a header. They called me back the next week and it went on from there, with them eventually offering me amateur terms.

It might not have been so, however. Indeed my career and the face of Merseyside football might have taken a different complexion had Liverpool had their way, for they were also keen to sign me as an amateur. In my heart I knew where I wanted to play, but I was still only a lad and I deferred to my dad on all significant matters in my life. Although he was from Salford and had taken me to see United, like all the best people I think there was a bit of Evertonian in him, and he told me to sign for the Blues.

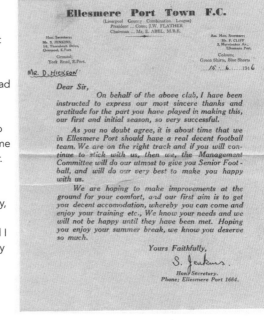

There was no glamour or fortune attached to being a young amateur player. Everton gave me a couple of pounds now and then to cover my bus fare, but that was about it. I was still allowed to play for and train with Ellesmere Port Town, which suited me fine because I just loved being on the pitch. There was no training organised by Everton, I did all that at Ellesmere Port and just crossed over the water when Everton asked me to play matches.

Although the chances of making it as a professional were so slim that we never really considered it a possibility, there were some very talented lads who would follow me through every one of Everton's various teams. Tony McNamara, who was three weeks older than me, was a stylish wing prodigy who would supply many of the crosses that I would bundle into the net from the C team to the first team, in which he made more than a century of appearances. In 1957 he took a path that I myself would unexpectedly follow a couple of years later by swapping Goodison for Anfield. Spells with Crewe and Bury during that same 1957/58 season meant that he became the first man to ever play in all four divisions in a single campaign.

The left back Jimmy Tansey was another talented local lad who would play more than a century of first-team games for Everton. Like me, he came up through the ranks as a wartime amateur and broke into the team when we were in the Second Division. He was a natural leader, always talking, cajoling, trying to do his best for Everton. Although the Everton teams we played in were not the most successful, we all had a winning mentality about us.

Six months younger than me was Tommy Jones, another local defender. He was a centre half who could also play in the left-back berth; a gentleman and leader, who had the difficult task of establishing himself in the first team in the season Everton were relegated. I was fortunate enough to miss that humiliation due to my national service! Tommy picked himself up, dusted himself down and went on to serve as Everton captain for many years.

I played because I enjoyed it, but I was a winner, definitely a winner; I wanted to win. Not at all costs, but enough. I was disappointed when we lost but then you looked forward to the next game. Training was hard going. We'd run laps of the pitch, lots of laps, with some heading practice and skills work, but not much else. People say that the game is fast now, but it was fast back then; it was fast in training and it was hard. You had to look after yourself on the training ground, just as you did on the pitch. There was no discussion about tactics, we worked all that out ourselves.

As I grew older and stepped up from the Everton C team to the B team and then the A team, my appearances for Ellesmere Port Town became less frequent, although I still trained there. I still had my job at Bowater's filling my days and most of my other teammates had work duties to fulfil as well, so for training we were largely left to our own devices. We played our games at Bellefield on Saturdays, but sometimes during the week as well. It was a simple life, but a good one.

Theo Kelly was the Everton manager during those years. He had risen through the club administration and, having originally been secretary-manager, was given charge of team affairs ahead of the ill-fated 1939/40 season. He had a reputation as a meddler and for falling out with the club's top players. Dixie Dean, Joe Mercer, Tommy Lawton and later T.G. Jones – some of the greatest players in Everton history – all left after falling foul of Theo.

Perhaps because I was only a kid I never saw that side to him. He was always fine with me, although at that stage we really had little interaction with the people running the club. In fact Kelly probably helped me and some of the others in turning professional. Under his management Everton were more concerned with bringing in the best local players and giving them a chance than buying in stars from elsewhere. At a board meeting in December 1947, just over a month after my eighteenth birthday, there was a resolution passed to strengthen this policy:

> **In view of the possible danger of losing good amateurs, due to 'poaching', it was felt that the Secretary should have the power to offer them part-time engagements commensurate with their age, as professionals.**

What this meant was that my days at the paper mill were coming to an end. The few quid that was given to me by the club every now and then to help with my fares was replaced by a weekly wage for playing football. Yes, I was finally being paid to play the game I loved! It wasn't much though! My first pay packet was the grand sum of £3 per week. At the end of the season, along with Jimmy Tansey and George Rankin, I was signed on as a professional for the 1948/49 season. I, however, wouldn't be pulling on a blue shirt for a while. Instead I was bound for distant shores.

I had been lucky during the war. I was too young to be called up to fight myself and my dad had avoided the fighting as well. Life, as I've written, was difficult, but could have been far more so. The war ended when I was 15, but there was no let-up on the demands facing Britain's young men. All healthy males aged between 17 and 21 were expected to serve in the armed forces for a minimum of 18 months, a situation that continued until 1960.

My call-up came when I was 18. Given that Britain still maintained an empire that stretched across Africa, the Middle East and Asia I could have been sent anywhere, or I could have spent the time in barracks down the road. For Everton that would have been the perfect situation.

In fact my first months as a conscript in 1948 presented the ideal scenario for my new employers. I was posted to the Cheshire Army Cadets in Chester, so I was far from neither home nor Merseyside. Not only that, when I was with the regiment's football team, I had a very special coach: Dixie Dean.

As a young Everton centre forward in the late 1940s I don't think you could want for a better mentor than somebody who a generation earlier had scored 60 league goals in a single season. Dixie was great. As a coach he was all right, but he was a devil for heading. I'd train with him and he'd

show me how he used to practise with a medicine ball. They'd put it on a rope in the gym and you used to have to jump up and head it. Then they'd raise the rope higher and you'd go at it again; that way you'd perfect your leap and increase the power in your heading.

As a kid I'd followed Dixie's own boyhood routine. He'd toss the ball up onto a roof. As it tumbled down the side of the roof, it was unseen to him until the very last moment and he would have a fraction of a second to position himself in order to meet it with his head. I did exactly the same and it honed my early ability.

We had some good times together while I was on national service. Dixie

took us over to Ireland to play some matches – we played Cliftonville, who were a top side over there. The story is that it was Dixie who recommended me to Everton, but that's not true. I'd already been there for nearly four years off and on by the time our paths crossed.

After my experience being coached by him while I was on national service, I got to know Dixie better when he was a publican in Chester in the 1950s. I used to pop into The Dublin Packet, where he had all his caps and medals on display, and have a little chat with him. Later, when I was also a retired footballer, I used to take him around to all the charity matches. He'd kick off the game (I'd usually be playing!) and afterwards we'd go back to his house, a little place in Rock Ferry, and have a drink.

This happy association came to an end sooner than either I or Everton would have liked. I was transferred over to the North Staffordshire Infantry Regiment and posted to Egypt. Theo Kelly was not in the least bit happy about this and tried everything he could to get me out of it and wrote many letters to all sorts of people trying to get me posted in England. Although I'd travelled around a bit playing football and visiting family in Salford, I'd never been anywhere and certainly not overseas (apart from Dixie's trips to Ireland). It was my duty to go, but at the same time I only wanted to play football.

In fact, I was on the boat bound for Egypt while Everton officials were still trying to get me out of travelling! It was all to no avail, however, and I was Suez bound. I'd remain in the Middle East until I was 20, rising to the rank of corporal.

I wouldn't ever say national service was my wake-up to the world because it was just not my scene. I wanted to get back to football. Had Everton got me off the boat I believe I would have started earlier in the first team.

It was hot and very different in Egypt and we never got any rain at all. Most of my time was spent on sentry duty and we had storehouses from which the Egyptians would try and steal stuff. It was my job to watch out for that. It wasn't very interesting, but it's what everybody had to do. We still had football though, and we sometimes played the locals – we called it their national team – in their bare feet. That was really enjoyable, but looking back it was all just an interruption on my rise to playing in the First Division, and you could never be too happy about that.

When I returned to England in January 1950 my wages at Everton had gone up to £8 per week, but the club was in a bad way. Theo Kelly had

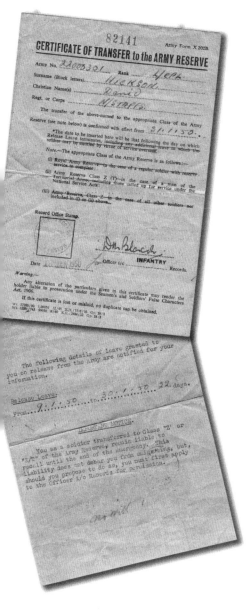

National service – as with so many of his teammates – interrupted Dave's career. Below: On tour with Everton in Germany.

reverted to being Everton secretary in September 1948 after a disastrous run of results at the start of the 1948/49 season (3–3, then 0–4, 0–1, 0–5, 0–5, 2–1, 0–6, 0–1) and was replaced by Cliff Britton.

Cliff had been a pre-war half back at Everton, winning the Second Division title in 1931 and the 1933 FA Cup as well as nine England caps. I remembered him when I first came into the club during the war. He was a fine player, a great reader of the game and for England had formed a famous defensive line with my fellow Portites, Joe Mercer and Stan Cullis, in wartime internationals.

I can't ever remember Cliff getting stripped off into his kit and joining us on the pitch at Bellefield, though. He was a collar-and-tie man, watching us from the edge of the pitch in his coat and suit. Cliff would usually get Gordon Watson to do the training with us. He had been a utility man in the late 1930s, winning a League Championship medal in 1939, and would fill all sorts of roles at Goodison over the years. Charlie Leyfield, who had been a winger during the 1930s, also used to help with the training.

Harry Cooke was the main one who used to look after us in those days. He was the top man at the time: kit man, physio and trainer rolled into one. He was very strict with the players, very meticulous and very fussy, sorting all the boots out and making sure everything would be ready. He had been a player with Everton 50 years earlier and had seen everything and knew everyone. Sometimes he used to tell us stories about the old days; names like Dixie, Chedgzoy, Sharp and Troup. His grandson, also Harry, joined later on as chief scout, although he was very different and would deal more with the board.

Cliff had turned around Everton's fortunes in that difficult 1948/49 season and we finished comfortably clear of relegation. However, his attempts to rebuild the Everton squad had not been successful and a similar group of players laboured to eighteenth in the 1949/50 campaign, winning just ten games. Although their league form wasn't great, there was some good in that team. They reached the 1950 FA Cup semi-final after an epic run, but fell to Liverpool.

'There are no personalities in the present-day Everton,' wrote the *Liverpool Echo's* correspondent 'Ranger' of this side. They did, however, possess 'a do-or-die spirit which is overcoming teams chock full of personality'. But things got even worse the next season.

I was playing regularly in the reserves by this stage. I'd made an impression in the traditional Blues v. Whites match between the first team and reserves in August 1950, coming on at half-time and scoring a hat-trick. 'Hickson, who came in at centre forward during the second half, recorded a hat-trick and it was the way he took his goals that pleased,' wrote the *Liverpool Echo* reporter, 'Stork'. I had no inkling of it at the time, but I was being watched by several lower-league clubs, such as York City, who tried to buy me from the club. The Everton board minutes record that the directors felt I had 'definite possibilities' and so held on to me.

During this time I often played with Alex Stevenson, who had made his name in the Dean and Lawton eras. Although he was coming to the end of his career he was a good little player. I often played in a forward line with him and Harry Catterick, whose natural position was centre forward but who played as inside left to accommodate me. Off the pitch Stevenson was a great character and one of the jokers in the dressing room.

Relegation hurt Everton very badly. It was a terrible thing for the club and luckily one that they've not had to encounter since. Even as a youngster you could sense the hurt from the first-team players. I hadn't

GIVEN SOCKS—BUT THEY CAN KEEP

Goals by try-again
...weep Villa
f the Cup

GERRY LOFTUS

...king a second come-back with Middlesbrough, £10,000 price-tag—and put his club in the F.A.

...e highlights of a 3—0 victory over Aston Villa in the ...land-road, Leeds.

...gned from Charlton as ...ot keep his place in the ...as tried at centre for-

...t inside left, Alec looks ...tional Ivor Powell could ...e and again his body ...ve minutes, was perfect ...la recovery from a first

...er, McCrae dashed down ...t Con Martin the wrong ...rds he advanced, then ...er Rutherford.

...e had scored the first ...l after twenty minutes ...th smart opportunism. ...the Villa defence ...tered he dashed through ...d took Linacre's pass and ...ored with a fierce drive. ...Middlesbrough were ...ways on top. Johnny ...buhler, deputy centre for-...ard, was a continual ...enace to the Villa defence.

The second goal came two minutes before the interval, when Mannion, taking Walker's pass, scored rather luckily from an acute angle.

Failure of the Villa wing ...alves left their forwards ...ith no scope, and when ...owe was injured half an ...our from time, the attack ...ad no combination.

Ronnie Dicks looks to be ...nother Boro' full back ...ho will play for England. Middlesbrough are away ...o Chesterfield in the ...ourth Round on January ...8.

HE WILL BE AT HOME AGAINST THE SWISS

WALTER RICKETT, Sheffield Wednesday and former Blackpool outside left, will deputise for Jimmy Mullen, of Wolves, in the England "B" team against Switzerland on his club's ground tomorrow.

Mullen has withdrawn because of an ankle injury but may be fit for the League game against Everton on Saturday.

Wolves' right back Kelly, who pulled a groin muscle at Middlesbrough on Saturday, may be out of the game for two weeks.

Carlisle United are seeking a left back. Manager Bill Shankly will watch Coventry's weekly practice match today before bidding for Bell, their twenty-four-year-old defender.

DAVE'S 5-GOAL PROMOTION BID

Dave Hickson was demobbed from the Army last week, but he looks like getting promotion just the same.

Dave, the centre forward Everton signed just before he entered the Services, played his first real game in eighteen months for the "A" team—and scored five goals in his side's 11—1 win against U.C.B. St. Helens. And he doesn't start training at Goodison Park until today.

His first step up is almost certain inclusion in the Everton Central League team on Saturday

NEWSBOY'S SELECTIONS

★ 1.0, Blue Duster; 1.30, Leal's Bouquet; 2.0, Ivon Louis de Belford; 2.30, Rowland Roy; 3.0, Mr. Fitz*; 3.30, Laverstoke. DOUBLE: Blue Duster and Mr. Fitz (nap).

Form Hints by Bouverie

1.0, Lion's Roar; 1.30, Eldoret*; 2.0, Kelek; 2.30, Coloured School Boy; 3.0, Mr. Fitz; 3.30, Bronze Boy. DOUBLE.—Eldoret (nap) ★and Kelek.

Jean Stuart's 2

2.30, Coloured School Boy; 3.30, Chasseur.

003 Kilbelin Bay, 12-1 F. Lewis ... Smith
.00 Cliss-Cottage, 11-12 Turnell
003 Chasseur, 11-12 McMorrow
003 Persian Glory, 11-12 ... T. Molony
000 Pegase III, 11-12 ....Trois Moulins 11-12 ... Mr. Parker
Highwayman 11-12

MUSTAQ ALI LEADS RECOVERY

INDIA fought back after losing three wickets cheaply in the fourth unofficial Test at Cawnpore and at the close of play yesterday had made 274 for five in reply to the Commonwealth first total of 448.

Mustaq Ali led the Indian recovery with a graceful 129 before being bowled by Frank...

Derek Mayers

Derek Mayers was a home-grown goalscoring outside right who made 19 appearances for Everton over five seasons in the mid-1950s. He found success at Preston North End, where he played alongside the immortal Tom Finney and almost lifted the League Championship. Later he had spells at Leeds, Bury and Wrexham.

You got what you saw with Dave. He was up in front of you all the time; he'd die for Everton. The main memories I have of him was him nodding balls on for me, when I scored a couple on my debut against Bury in 1953.

I played on the wing, and those days you had to stay on your wing; nowadays they rotate and go all over the pitch, but not then; you had to stay on your wing.

I played under two very different managers at Everton. Personally I thought Cliff Britton was a good manager, a great manager. He later signed me for Preston and we finished runners-up in the 1957/58 in the First Division, if you can call that success. We never got anything for it, not even a medal.

The man who succeeded him, Ian Buchan, was a fitness training instructor at Loughborough College. I think he was professor of something or other, but he didn't know an awful lot about football. I can remember one time, we played Chelsea at Goodison. We got beaten 3–0, and he said, 'I'm not going to talk to you now, lads; I'll see you at Bellefield on Monday, we'll sort it all out then.' I'm not kidding, nothing went right. Pre-plan free-kicks went wrong, throw-ins went wrong; nothing went right at all, so we thought we're going to get a right bollocking at Bellefield. On Monday we got down there and we all gathered in the practice room, and Ian comes in and says, 'Well, lads, I've thought a lot about that game on Saturday, and for the life of me I can't think where we went wrong!' We all fell about laughing. Everything was wrong and he couldn't even see it.

You could have a good laugh with Dave. I remember we used to have a snooker room up at Everton where the lads would go to after they'd finished training in the morning. Dave used to play a little, and sometimes when he was halfway through a game some of the lads would shout 'Ho!' and everybody would grab the snooker balls and run out of the room! Dave used to do his nut and break cues and all sorts. There were wood-panelled walls at Everton, and we used to put the broken cues behind the back of the wood so they wouldn't find them.

All that said, Dave was usually quite a mild-mannered man off the field. On it you could see he was like a red rag to a bull. He'd run through a brick wall. Referees used to tolerate a lot of things in those days. It was tough, but there was no biting people or anything like that; you couldn't get away with that.

Dave was every bit as committed in training as he was in games. We used to play head tennis on a little pitch at the back of Gwladys Street. We'd play for a few bob or a pound, which was quite a lot in those days. But dear me; the air went blue when he lost.

played any part in the disastrous run-in, although I had been selected as twelfth man for a visit to Charlton Athletic in March 1951. Back in those days, twelfth man really was twelfth man; we used to push the skips in and help the trainer. There was no substitutes and no chance of getting on the field, unless someone was unexpectedly injured or taken ill in the build-up to the game.

Despite their problems I was still in awe of Everton. I wanted to play and I was determined I was going to make it. I knew they didn't belong in the Second Division and I wanted to help them. We were under no illusions that the task facing us was going to be hard. Just two teams went up in those days and there were no play-offs. Financially football was run on a much more equal basis, so that big clubs – and we were one of the biggest, despite relegation – found it harder to acquire players from elsewhere. Certainly this was a problem Cliff Britton came up against.

Everton's spell in the Second Division started on Saturday 18 August 1951 against Southampton at The Dell. My contemporary T. E. Jones had broken into the first team the previous ill-fated season and was starting at centre back. Ted Sagar, a remnant of the glory years first of Dean, then Lawton, was in goal. The rest of the line-up that day was Eric Moore, Jock Lindsey, Jackie Grant, Cyril Lello, Ted Buckle, Harry Potts, Peter Farrell, Tommy Eglington and, wearing the number nine shirt that I coveted, Harry Catterick.

Because he was so successful as Everton manager a decade later, people tend to talk down Harry's qualities as a player. He was all right, was Harry, a good centre forward. He had scored a few goals in previous seasons, despite never really being able to call the number nine shirt his own. He was a bit older than the rest of us and had missed a lot of football because of the war, but you could see some of the leadership qualities that marked him out as a manager a few years later.

I was twelfth man that day. We lost 1–0 down on the south coast and although we beat Brentford the following

Wednesday, a draw against Sheffield Wednesday and defeat in the return fixture at Griffin Park on the August Bank Holiday Monday led to mutterings of discontent.

Everything that was going wrong for the first team, however, was going right for the reserves. Forty-eight hours after the Brentford defeat I was selected to play centre forward against Sheffield Wednesday reserves in a Central League match. It was great playing for the reserves and we always had good gates, because we played at Goodison. We won 7–1 in that game, and I scored five times. The following Saturday I was picked for my first-team debut, away at Leeds United, in place of Harry Catterick. Poor Harry never played for Everton again.

Back in those days the manager would post the team on the dressing room door the day before the match. I was so delighted when I saw my name up there. It went into the evening paper and people coming to the game would know who was playing. You wouldn't do that now! In the dressing room on the day of the match was a pile of telegrams from well-wishers, including my Mum, Dad and Peter, as well as another name known by all Evertonians. 'Good luck son,' it read, 'Dixie.'

We played well at Elland Road on a day on which Tony McNamara also made his debut. It was a place where generations of Everton teams would struggle, but we always did all right there. Tommy Eglington scored two goals that day, and I laid on his second. I always liked setting up my teammates, almost as much as I did scoring.

The reports in the local press were generally quite promising after my debut. 'Hickson,' reported the *Echo*, 'showed ideas, although up against a strong centre half.' Its chief correspondent, Ranger, wrote prophetically, 'I think the time will come, though not this season, and maybe not next, when Everton will have a team capable of having a long spell of success. This will be when the present young players … have absorbed experience and been nursed to stardom.'

The following Wednesday I kept my place in the team to make my full Goodison debut, against Nottingham Forest. John Willie Parker, with whom I would form such a good partnership over coming years, scored the only goal of the game as we recorded our third victory of the season. 'Hickson is a grand worker and wholehearted trier, and though he has much to learn, looks quite promising,' reported the *Echo*. 'He can certainly hustle the defence more than somewhat.'

On his return from national service Dave was given a new contract by Everton, with wages of £8 per week.

On Saturday I scored my first goal for the club, when we drew 3–3 at home to Rotherham United. The strike came on nine minutes when Harry Potts' shot was parried by the Rotherham keeper into my path. I hit the ball home from nine yards and my Everton career was fully under way. 'Hickson,' wrote the *Echo*, 'was Everton's most dangerous forward. He gave [Alf] Gibson and the backs a rare running about, and chased even the most remote chance with a Liddell-like determination.' In his column the following Monday – entitled 'The Shape of Things to Come. Pointers to Future Prospects' – Ranger wrote, 'Hickson obviously requires a few rough corners smoothed off before he fills the bill entirely, but he has promise, and is the type likely to harass opposing defences more than some leaders, for he is no slave to orthodox ideas.'

We finished the 1951/52 season seventh in the Second Division and would end the following season sixteenth, the lowest overall position – 38th – in Everton's history. I ended my debut campaign with 14 goals, my second with 16, 12 of which came in the league. Despite doing well myself, I don't know why we found it hard as a team in the Second Division. I think struggle is the wrong word, but we never looked like we were going down again. It always seemed like we were getting it together, but it obviously took time. There were a few young players like me, and I suppose you're learning all the time. Sometimes you need to have that bit of experience to push you over the line.

There were times when we'd play exceptionally well and just not get the result we needed. I remember one game in the season that we finished sixteenth in the Second Division and chance after chance after chance came our way. It was unbelievable. And somehow we ended up losing 1–0. We were the best team, but that's what can happen.

Nobody ever pointed fingers, or accused teammates of not being good enough or pulling their weight. It wasn't the Everton way. Everyone gave 100 per cent on the pitch and to each other.

The supporters were always brilliant; they always stuck by us. They could see that we were trying our best for Everton and respected that. If it was quiet you tended not to take any notice, but if they got behind you it really used to encourage you. They were great, even when we were in the middle of the Second Division. They were patient and never heckled. They could see that we were trying to play good, exciting football. Sometimes when we went away you'd get booed or heckled by the home fans before kickoff. But that was only because they knew we were going to have a go.

Cliff Britton probably bore the brunt of supporter frustrations. It's a shame because he had been a good player for Everton and was a nice man. But it was hard getting out of the Second Division. It was hard to play in. I never felt like it was any easier scoring in the second tier than when I played in the top flight. There were only two promotion slots and none of this play-off business you have nowadays. Now, if you're in the top ten or twelve by Easter, you're still in with a chance of going up, but there was none of that then.

That said, the pressure facing players and managers in the 1950s was nothing like it is today. I don't know what's going on now, with the TV and mobile phones and computers, with news on

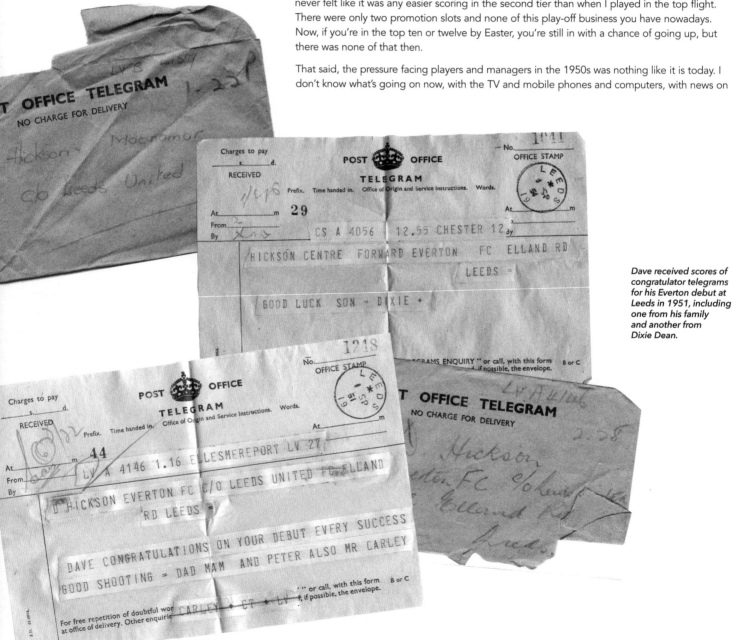

Dave received scores of congratulator telegrams for his Everton debut at Leeds in 1951, including one from his family and another from Dixie Dean.

all the time. The things that are going on in football today are unbelievable. The attention and pressure facing everyone is incredible. It's hard. How would I have fared in the 21st-century environment? I'd have loved it. Oh yeah, I'd have loved it.

In the dressing room we all stuck together. There was never any finger pointing, or feeling that someone wasn't pulling his weight or wasn't good enough. Nobody ever said to Cliff, 'We should be signing this fella.' It's not like it is today with all the transfer talk and speculation. We had no subs or anything, just the eleven players that were changed by Cliff very infrequently. It helped build up a great team spirit.

I was fearless. Nothing scared or overawed me. I played against some of the greatest defenders there were, like Billy Wright, and also some of the hardest, like Malcolm Barrass. I feared neither type of player. The fearlessness I had in my game was something that was always in me. Off the pitch people tell me I'm quite mild, but on it I just had an absolutely unbelievable desire to win, to score goals. I just wanted to finish; to finish a move with the ball in the back of the net. It was determination, it was never anything personal. When it's all over you shake hands and that's it.

Nobody likes getting kicked or punched, but it's what happened in football in the 1950s. As long as we never broke someone's legs, you were okay – and we never did that at Everton. You would go for the ball and the man. It was a hard game, but a good and exciting game. I think it's gone a little too far the other way now. I think the players are too quick to go over and the referees too quick to penalise.

Why was I so brave? Firstly, because I wanted to win. But also because I loved the game. I think, looking back, I loved it too much – if it's possible to love anything too much. I just wanted to be out there on the pitch, playing, succeeding, winning. I lived football and I loved Everton. I became really obsessed by them, as I am today. I might be 83 now, but I still play every week with the lads. I'm up there in the stands, playing every single ball. I might do the PR now, but as far as I'm concerned I'm still playing – if only in my own head. There's nobody more gutted than me if we lose.

Don Roberts

Growing up in Ellesmere Port, Don Roberts was a family friend of the Hicksons. He knew many of the local professional footballers in the area, but it was Dave who left the greatest impression.

I was an apprentice butcher in the shop that his mum used to come in to, and every day Dave would come in and say 'hello' before he went to Goodison, and consequently we got quite friendly. His Mum was a big client of ours; I knew them quite well. In later years he came to Ellesmere Port Town as manager; my brother Ted was a groundsman there, and they developed a friendship.

I'm a few years younger than Dave and I didn't know him at school but I knew a lot of his friends. Even when he was very young he was a bit of an idol. He learned his football off a centre forward at Ellesmere Port Town called Pongo Waring, an older fellow. The last time I saw him we were reminiscing about Pongo.

Ellesmere Port had a great football heritage. Joe Mercer, of course, was the most famous player from the town. I think Joe Mercer had a lot to do with encouraging Dave to get where he was. Stan Cullis, he lived at the opposite end of the street to myself. I lived in 87 Oldfield Road and he lived in number 1. Of course, I didn't see a lot of him because he was with Wolves at the time. I didn't know much about Sam Chedgzoy, another famous Ellesmere Port footballer, to be quite honest with you; I know the name.

Dave was a very approachable figure. He didn't have a car when he was a young man, and he used to get the bus every morning, outside the premises where I worked.

I've been going to see Everton since 1946. I was originally taken by my brothers – I was the youngest of seven. When they were in the Second Division the standard of football was very different to the top flight but they always had that attitude about them that they were going to do well. Of course, it was in my heart so I couldn't see what was wrong with it. Sometimes the supporters got a wee bit frustrated. Like everything in life, you have your ups and downs, but they'd forgive and forget anything that went on. However, I remember them playing Sunderland and they were all on about Davey and there was nearly a ruction caused because some of the supporters were condemning him for his attitude, while others liked that he got stuck in. He was a gentleman through and through, though, a different person on the pitch to how he was off it.

My brother said Dave was an awkward old sausage, but he was a fantastic footballer and a fantastic person. As a manager he was a very strict person for the rules, but he also did the same thing at Ellesmere Port Town as Neville Southall later did at Goodison – he sat in the centre of the pitch to object to something the referee did or some bloody player not playing well. He just sat down and was very awkward!

The 1952/53 season started with optimism that we'd pull ourselves out of the Second Division, a place where a club like Everton has no place being. 'With their big army of former schoolboy and county youth stars Everton should be able to produce a side not only capable of putting them back in the top section, but keeping them there in a comfortable position,' wrote Ranger in the *Liverpool Echo* on the eve of the new season. 'I feel that the club will be well in the

winning the League Championship.

We hadn't done so well in my first experience of the FA Cup, losing a third round replay at home to Leyton Orient. Second time around, in 1952/53, we did much better. Indeed, the run has gone down in Everton history and my part in it is something I became famous for.

We were fortunate to have home ties in the third and fourth round. Ipswich Town were seen off 3–2, and I got a couple of goals. Next were Nottingham Forest, who were in the same division as us, but higher up. We won that game 4–1 thanks to a brace by John Willie Parker and goals by

running for promotion this year, but have no feeling of certainty that they would actually pull it off. Judging on last season's displays, the side just lacks that little spark of combined genius and spirit which makes all the difference.'

It was to be one of the most dramatic campaigns in Everton history, but not for the right reasons in the league. We didn't start well, losing our first three games and scoring just once. We went to the bottom of the Second Division; the lowest point in Everton history. The mood was not very good at all. I never liked losing. Like me, my teammates wanted to get out there and win. But it was no good feeling sorry for ourselves. We just had to pick ourselves up, that was all.

As well as getting out of the Second Division, our other priority was doing as well as we could in the FA Cup. In the days before European football and the League Cup, and with international football still undeveloped, it was a huge thing in those days. In terms of prestige it was, in many people's minds, the equal of

Tommy Eglington and Tommy Clinton. That result led to a fifth round tie against Manchester United at Goodison Park.

The game on Valentine's Day was to go down as one of the most famous in Everton's history. It's the match that made my reputation, the one everyone remembers me for.

United, who were reigning League Champions, had a super side. The Irish international Johnny Carey, who was later my manager, was captain. Up front they had Jack Rowley. There was quality all through their ranks, players like Ray Wood, Roger Byrne, Johnny Berry and David Pegg. A massive crowd of 77,920 packed Goodison, an attendance that had been bettered just once before.

I came into the game in good form, having scored a hat-trick a week earlier against Brentford at Goodison. However, you didn't need any extra motivation or form for these sort of occasions. A crowd like that does it for you. It was a ferocious atmosphere. We wanted to repay Evertonians' faith, and they hadn't had much to cheer about for a long time.

Yet the game did not start as planned. United took a 27th-minute lead when Johnny Berry's shot was palmed by our goalie Jimmy O'Neill into the path of Jack Rowley, and he scored from six yards. I suppose then it looked like the game was going according to form. United's advantage was, however, short-lived. Seven minutes later I played in Tommy Eglington, who took it around Johnny Aston and let fly with a right-footed shot which flew into the back of the United net.

Five minutes from the interval came the moment everyone remembers. Jack Lindsay crossed and I dived in, trying to connect with his cross. In doing so I caught an opponent's boot and was left with blood streaming from a wound above my right eye. Harry Cooke led me from the field with a ball of cotton wool affixed to my head.

I missed the last few minutes of the first half as, in the dressing room, old Harry did his best to stop the bleeding before the doctor stitched the wound up and put a bandage on it during half-time. But I had to come back on. There was really no choice in the matter. I came onto the field after the break, a few seconds after my teammates. I'm sure there were some people there who didn't think I'd make it back out, but that was never an option.

Shortly after I returned, I headed against the post from a corner, which opened up the wound again. There was blood and all that everywhere. At this point the referee, Mr Beacock of Scunthorpe, suggested to Peter Farrell that I should leave the field.

'He'll have to go off,' said the referee. 'He can't go on with an eye like that. He's not normal.'

There was no way I was going off the pitch, no way at all.

'I am normal,' I told him. 'Tell him I'm normal, Peter, tell him!'

'Of course you are, Dave,' said Peter.

'There you are, ref!' I said. 'I'm staying!'

I was drenched in blood, but with the noise of the crowd and the sense of occasion I kept going. I had a couple of chances as did Ted Buckle.

On 63 minutes came the game's decisive moment. I took Tommy Eglington's pass on my chest, beat one man, sidestepped another and hammered a right-footed shot beyond the reach of Ray Wood and into the United net.

Goodison erupted in celebration. It was a wonderful moment. But there was still nearly a third of the game to go and I was going to fight until the end. I nearly set up John Willie Parker a couple of times, but my goal was enough to seal victory. At the end, Jimmy O'Neill ran the length of the pitch to congratulate me. Then they took me into the dressing room to stitch me up again. It was some game.

'Hickson,' wrote Ranger in the *Liverpool Echo*, 'gave a magnificent display of indomitable courage throughout the second half with blood streaming from a cut above the eye.'

He continued: 'Hickson was the man of the attack. His grit and determination … carried him through despite his handicap and he still chased the ball as though his very life depended on it. All one side of his face was covered with blood but still he kept pegging away. When the final whistle went O'Neill dashed half the length of the field to throw his arms around Hickson, the hero of a wonderful win, but one which was shared equally by all eleven players.'

Hickson's heroic performance against Manchester United was the defining performance of his career. It brought him national recognition for the first time and wrote his name into Goodison lore. Little did he know that it also brought him fame beyond these shores.

A few weeks later Torino made an inquiry about Hickson. Il Grande Torino had been European football's first great club of the post-war era, winning four consecutive Serie A titles and playing a revolutionary brand of football that utilised a 4-2-4 formation. When Italy played Hungary in May 1947 the Azzurri's line-up included no fewer than ten Torino players, plus the Juventus goalkeeper.

On 4 May 1949, on the brink of their fifth back-to-back title, the team were involved in a plane crash on their way back from a friendly against Benfica in Portugal. Nearly all members of the team and coaching staff were killed.

Torino were in the process of rebuilding when they moved for Hickson. Serie A was Europe's wealthiest league at the time and offered riches far beyond the meagre maximum wage allowed by the Football League.

It wasn't the first time that an Italian club had moved for an Everton player. In 1948 AS Roma had tried to buy T.G. Jones, offering to double his salary and provide him with a villa in Rome. That move had fallen down due to restrictions on currency exchange. Hickson's move to Torino never got that far. The Everton board summarily rejected the bid and it seems that they never told Hickson either.

Following the United game we travelled to Doncaster Rovers for a midweek league fixture. I was out injured after being bashed around in the United game, with John Willie playing at centre forward and Nobby Fielding coming into the side, but the heroes of the previous Saturday fell to a lame 3–0 defeat. Later in the season we'd play Huddersfield Town on successive days, beating them 2–1 at home, then losing 8–2 at their place 24 hours later. Everton were a team that could do that sort of thing in the 1950s. Even though we finished the 1952/53 season sixteenth in the Second Division, I could sense the improvement on the previous campaign. We were getting together a tremendous spirit and developing as a team.

Supporters also started to recognise that. An R.R. Knowles of Birkenhead wrote to the *Echo* after the United win: 'Having been highly critical in the past, may I now congratulate Everton on the vastly-improved displays given since, and including the game at Nottingham. The aggression, "bite", and general desire to go forward have been glorious to watch. Long may it continue, and may we see the Blues not only win at Villa Park, but go on to Wembley.'

The win over United saw us drawn at Aston Villa in the quarter-finals a fortnight later. It was a tough draw – Villa were in the First Division – and another big crowd, with more than 60,000 filling Villa Park, including many Evertonians.

It was a tight game and Villa had their chances. One thing about being a centre forward in those days was that you were only expected to attack. Now you see everyone coming back to defend set-pieces, but there was none of that really. So when, 15 minutes from the end, Everton launched a break, following a scrum in their own area, I was on hand to assist. The ball was hacked clear as far as me, just inside our own half. I switched play to Ted Buckle – who was in the outside-left position – and sprinted forward to take the return pass. Then, holding off the challenge of a Villa defender, I fired the ball home.

'For seventy-five minutes big Frank Moss, of Aston Villa, "played" Dave Hickson like an angler – like an angler scared stiff that his prize catch might get away. Then it happened. Hickson was away with rod, line and sinker, and Everton's magnificently vocal supporters were hailing the goal which made the difference,' reported Leslie Edwards in the following Monday's *Daily Post*.

'Hickson brushed [Moss] off like a crumb off a waistcoat, and closed to about ten yards. Then, as if this were something he was used to doing every minute of every day, he hit the kind of shot which wakes goalkeepers out of nightmare dreams. A perfect goal; timely, well-deserved, well-constructed and, as we thought, the end of all Villa's hopes.'

A few minutes later I 'scored' another a goal. It struck the underside of the bar and I'm sure it went over the line. The referee never gave it, but it didn't matter in the end. The final score was 1–0.

The crowd, as always, were fantastic. Quite a contingent had travelled down from Liverpool and at the final whistle they all came onto the pitch, hoisted me above their shoulders and carried me off. 'Crazed spectators climbed from the terraces in hundreds to swarm towards one player – Hickson,' wrote Edwards. 'They hugged him, kissed him, patted him, ruffled his tousled hair and became such an embarrassment to him that a solitary policeman was engulfed and Hickson was in danger of being killed by kindness.' It was a wonderful moment, but they've always been great to me, the Everton fans.

We were now high on confidence ahead of our semi-final tie against Bolton Wanderers at Maine Road. We didn't feel we had anything to fear from them, even if they had the England centre forward, Nat Lofthouse, up front. They were in the First Division, but had a reputation for being solid and workmanlike.

I don't know what went wrong in the first half of the semi. It wasn't that we were terrible, more that they just played exceptionally well and Lofthouse – who was a great, great player – was at the centre of everything. Before we knew it they were 4–0 up. Half the time I didn't know what was going on. I'd gone up for a ball that was heading for me and Malcolm Barrass, the Bolton centre half, flattened me. I don't know what had happened, whether it was on purpose or not. The ball was heading to me and next thing I was on the floor, gasping for air. I was really out of it and had to leave the field for 15 minutes. In fact I was only really half-fit for the rest of the game.

Shortly before half-time we had a glimmer of hope when a penalty was awarded in our favour. Tommy Clinton stepped up to take it, but could only send it wide of the Bolton goal. At that stage we were only looking to get some respectability. Little did we know then that that would probably be the game's decisive moment.

In the second half we pulled three goals back. John Willie Parker headed two goals and Peter Farrell scored from a free kick. But it wasn't enough. They beat us. It was a great match, but we missed out.

There was a feeling of devastation in the dressing room afterwards. I never usually looked back. I never reflected on what might have been. I always looked forward to the next game if we got beaten, but this was different. There were lads there that knew they'd never come so close to winning a trophy. I was one of them, it turned out. I never got so close in the FA Cup again after that.

My immediate disappointment, however, was dampened by my injuries. I was out of it. I went to stay with relatives in Manchester that night and they didn't recognise me. It was unbelievable. I'd been bashed around so badly in my face. My eyes were filled with blood for weeks and my mum wasn't happy about it at all. I remember watching on Pathé News a few days later being played through. I couldn't believe I missed it. I'm sure if it wasn't for the concussion

I'd have scored and brought us back into the game.

A close relative of one of Dave's teammates claimed that his condition was so bad following the beating that he'd taken from Barrass that after the final whistle he was hallucinating. 'We did it lads, we're going to Wembley!' Dave was heard exclaiming in the dressing room. He had to be calmed by his subdued colleagues.

Afterwards the pain gave way to real sadness. That's what happens. Whenever Everton do well in the cup I always think about that game and what might have been in 1953.

Bolton later played Blackpool in what became known as the Matthews Final, losing 4–3, the same scoreline by which they'd beaten us. I think we'd have won that game. We were good enough. I'll always regret never having the chance to have played at Wembley while I was a professional. It would have seen us make an indelible impression in Everton football history.

I think there's probably parallels between our team in the 1950s and Everton's teams in recent years. The brand of football that Everton played under the last few years of David Moyes's reign was fantastic. But when you'll look back in the future, I think a lot of the players won't get the credit they deserve because they never won a trophy. It was a little bit like the story of me and my time in the 1950s. We played good, exciting football; we came close to winning trophies on a few occasions, but we didn't get the credit for it.

Some of the players are a little bit bitter about being overlooked in such a way. Not all of them, but some are. I'm not just talking about those that played for Everton, but any team. I think you can have a really good team and just lack the finish – like Everton under Moyes. Because you fall short it doesn't make your career bad or ordinary; you just lacked that little something extra. Sometimes it was only down to luck.

Crowd gathered at Goodison after promotion secured in 1954. Hickson with Peter Farrell and Eddie Wainwright

After our FA Cup run and the disappointment of finishing so far down the Second Division there was a real resolve among us to get Everton back where they belonged in the top flight. We sat down at the start of the 1953/54 season and resolved to do it. I think the spirit was all over the club. We had improved and all the players were playing well together. You could see it was getting better and better all the time.

My partnership with John Willie Parker really took off that season. He was an excellent inside forward. We had a good working relationship and with that you always know what the other fellow is doing. Between us we scored 60-odd goals the season we went up. People always say that's great, but I always say, 'Well, Dixie scored sixty on his own!' Wally Fielding was a great player, don't get me wrong, but sometimes you didn't know what he was going to do. You'd expect it and he'd turn his back on you, when he should have played the first ball.

John Willie was really my partner in crime. We each knew what we were going to do; if I was going for a ball he'd be there waiting for it and I could find him. He was from Birkenhead and played for several years for Everton as an amateur before turning professional later on. We made our debuts around the same time, but he was more than four years older than me so was in his mid-twenties before he made his league bow.

Some people said he didn't move around enough, but for me he was always in and out of everywhere. He didn't really have pace, John. He had a long stride on him and he used to deceive people a lot. Ranger in the *Echo* got it right when he said that 'His deceptively lazy and nonchalant style lulls defenders into a false sense of security. By the time they wake up to it, it is usually too late.'

I used to love setting up chances for John Willie, but it takes two to make a partnership. It gave me great joy to set up chances for teammates; people often overlook that this is, after all, a team game. I could probably have scored more goals if I'd wanted to, if I'd been a bit more selfish, but I didn't. Helping others was always my priority. He gave me opportunities as well. He'd give me one goal and I'd give him one back. He was quite a guy was John Willie; a good worker and a real nice fella. He was one of the teammates I stayed in touch with after football and he ran a couple of pubs.

On 13 March 1954 his hat-trick in the last 15 minutes saw off Rotherham in front of a Goodison crowd of 52,000. That 3–0 victory left Everton top with just nine games left. We stumbled a little bit after that, but we were always within a point or two of promotion.

A crucial but often overlooked moment in that season's run-in came when we played Stoke City at Goodison with six games to go. Our left back was Jack Lindsay, and what a player he was. He was a big-money signing from Glasgow Rangers, and a really good player. In this particular game he broke his leg in a challenge that saved us a goal. It was a terrible injury, a double leg-break, and it could have finished him off. We drew 1–1 that day instead of losing and went up a few weeks later by a single point. Jack was out injured for two years and never played for Everton again. His sacrifice that day played a crucial part in our promotion.

A fortnight later we played Birmingham City at Goodison. Just short of 63,000 people turned out to see us, and I would score the only goal of the game. 'Hickson has scored many extremely valuable goals for Everton, but none of greater significance than his splendid header at the 38th minute against Birmingham,' reported the *Liverpool Echo*. 'Had it not been for that goal, we should not now be caring two straws about the game at Oldham, as Everton's promotion chances would have been extinguished.'

For the final match of the season we went to bottom-placed Oldham on a Thursday evening. Everton were in third place behind Leicester City on 56 points and Blackburn Rovers on 55. With both of those sides having completed their programme of fixtures, it meant that we needed a win against Oldham at Boundary Park to pull level with Leicester and pip Blackburn to promotion. If we scored six, we would be crowned Second Division Champions.

They say there were 20,000 Scousers there that night, but I thought it was nearly 40,000. You'd never normally get that at Oldham, would you? They said that they tarmacked over everywhere – literally poured hot sticky tar over the walls – to stop people getting in, but it didn't work. The fans climbed over everything to get in. The place was packed, heaving. It was a fantastic night.

We were 4–0 up at half-time. Tommy Jones and I each scored one – Tommy getting his with a shot from our half – and John Willie a brace, but we still needed two more to win the Second Division Championship. Tommy Eglington hit the post and our old teammate George Burnett,

who was in goal for Oldham, kept a few out. We had a great chance to go clear of Leicester, but it wasn't to be. The score remained stuck at 4–0. We hadn't won the Championship, but we'd been promoted.

At the final whistle, not for the first time in my career, hundreds of Everton supporters invaded the pitch and carried us off the field. We had a celebration in the dressing room and photos taken, before getting the bus home and going our separate ways. Everton were back in the First Division and – although there were a few scares against Wimbledon and Coventry in the 1990s – they've stayed there ever since.

It was the highlight of my career. Even now when people stop me and say, 'Hi, Davey,' I think it's because they look back at the time when we got them back up to where they are now. I think people remember that time, even if they weren't around to see it or experience it. Evertonians are very good with their history and there's a sense of recognition that I was part of a side that got them back to where they belong. They've been very close to going down again a few times, but they've got through it. I'm proud that Everton have sat in the top flight for six decades following our efforts.

I always consider it a great team effort, but many singled me out for praise. Ranger wrote this about me after our promotion was secured:

I firmly believe that without Hickson Everton would not have gained promotion. He has embodied in his strong and resolute body and pugnacious temperament, more fighting spirit than the rest of the forward line put together.

Not only has Hickson a great chance next season to prove that he can claim to rank among the best of modern centre-forwards on pure footballing ability, as apart from robust fighting displays, but if he sets himself out to do it he can succeed far beyond the expectations of those who are ready to write him down as a player of one type only.

In some ways we found the First Division easier than the second tier. Early in the 1954/55 season we went top, and although form dipped, it rose again too. After a slow start personally, goals continued to come the way of John Willie and me. Our partnership made such a promising start in the top flight that with ten games left that season, Everton moved up to fourth, four points behind league leaders Chelsea, and with three games in hand.

'Everton have struck a solid blow for common sense in football management,' reported the *Liverpool Echo*. 'Not a penny has been spent on transfer fees since they suffered relegation and the club has proved that sound planning and a long-term policy, allied in good coaching and a loyal staff, can be just as effective in staging a come-back as handing out big sums for ready-made players.'

I think we were probably undone by our lack of experience in the end. We lost seven, drew two and won just one of our remaining fixtures, finishing the season eleventh – the lowest position we'd held all year.

Even at the height of his powers Dave Hickson fiercely divided opinions. For a support schooled on the sublimely talented Tommy Lawton and the goalscorer supreme, Dixie Dean, he represented a different kind of player: fearless, yes, but rough, aggressive, contrary. Sometimes his passion came across as petulant. Yet his supporters were devoted and defended him.

An exchange in the *Daily Post* in February 1954 between a reader – Mr J. Timson of Stoneycroft – and correspondent Leslie Edwards was a good exposition of the issues at stake.

'Recently you [*Daily Post*] seem to have become anti-Hickson,' wrote Mr Timson. 'Whenever you report on Everton you cannot resist having a dig at him. While I agree he is robust, I do think you are inclined to lay all the blame on him. Yet at times he is more sinned against than sinning. For instance, I was present at the game at Sheffield on Saturday. Hickson was very harshly treated, indeed, and although he was provoked he did not lose his head. Further he refused to be intimidated (surely this proves his courage and greatness?).'

Leslie Edwards replied: 'I have no crusade against Hickson. Indeed I am continually defending him and suggesting that he is a far better footballer than many critics imagine. But I do crusade (and shall) against foul play.

'Traditional Everton style scarcely needs recalling. Everywhere football is played spectators went to see Everton teams confident that they would get scientific artistic football played within the spirit, and letter, of the laws of the game, No one ever suggested Everton's years of glory were produced by teams playing over-robustly.

'On the contrary. Hickson is effective, enthusiastic, unselfish and talented. But enthusiasm sometimes out-runs discretion, and that is a bad thing.'

A month later a similar exchange ran through the pages of the *Liverpool Echo*, with Ranger having to deny accusations that he was 'anti-Hickson', but criticising the forward's petulance.

'His temperament being what it is, vigorous and robust play comes naturally to him. Nobody objects to that. Indeed, his grim determination and unconquerable fighting spirit have had much to do with Everton's success this season.

'Unfortunately, the line of demarcation between the honest and permissible employment of every ounce of nerve, muscle and sinew and the descent into questionable retaliatory tactics is sometimes very easily overstepped. Hickson, in short, is in danger of becoming one of Soccer's "marked men" in more than one sense of the term.

'I am not anti-Hickson. Far from it. But I feel that in his own interests Hickson should make a real endeavour to curb his impetuosity, for the benefit of his side as well as himself. I firmly believe that by doing so he will not only be a better player individually, but a better team man as well.

'I know it is easy to sit in the stand and criticise, but not so easy to submit to some things in the heat of the moment on the field of play. But let the field of play be one of play, not of "battle", and let Hickson be less ready to "have a go" at those who have a go at him. If he does not take these words to heart, which are meant in a helpful sense, he may have cause for regret.'

Mrs K. Jones of Emerald Street, Liverpool 6, replied acerbically: 'You have been nothing more than a Hickson critic this past season. You have definitely got Anfield Relegation Fever, and the only way you can bring your temperature down is to pull Hickson to pieces … We like Dave the way he is, so let him alone.'

Ranger's riposte was equally cutting: 'Just as there are more ways of killing a pig than choking it with butter, so there are more avenues to victory than by laying about all and sundry as though "possessed".'

As Hickson's fame rose, following promotion to the top flight, so, alas, did his notoriety. Journalists singled him out in their columns for criticism, and referees were quick to stamp down on his antics. His supporters remained as adoring as his critics were strident. He would receive dozens of letters – which he kept for the rest of his life – from fans bemoaning the injustices he faced week in week out, and imploring management, officials, journalists, to give him a fair deal.

Supporters also begged Hickson to take it easy, for there was a feeling that his poor disciplinary record was undermining his potential. 'I would like you to make up your mind that no how much you get needled you will not retaliate,' wrote J. D. Newton of Magazine Lane, Wallasey, in November 1954. 'THAT I know is a terrific thing to ask a man with red blood in his veins, but I ask you to do this for one reason David. IF you can (and from now on all eyes will be on you). I say within two years you will be PLAYING FOR YOUR COUNTRY.' He enclosed a copy of a letter defending Hickson written to the Daily Express's Henry Rose, but added that his most recent display had made him look 'a bit of a clot' in his defence to the journalist. 'All the best my lad,' he concluded, 'And don't forget your battle cry, "I will not lose my hair."' That, at least, was one thing the immaculately bequiffed Hickson could never be accused of.

What was being a footballer like in the 1950s? What was it like to be an Everton player?

I was living the dream, getting paid to play a sport I really loved – loved perhaps a bit too much – and for a team that I loved too.

While some things are similar – the family ethos at Everton, for example – most aspects of the game were almost unimaginably different.

After Theo Kelly left the club in the early 1950s Bill Dickinson took over as secretary and was responsible for most of the running of the club. What was Everton like as an institution back then? It was well run, efficient, strict on a lot of matters, but it was also a family club. It's always been a family club. When David Moyes came in, he described it as 'the People's Club of Merseyside'. He emphasised then what I'd known for 60-odd years. It's all true.

I think that's why so many of my teammates retained such a strong affinity for Everton, and you can still see this rubbing off on the players now. Look at Leighton Baines. To me he's Man of the Match nearly every week at Everton; he's a fantastic player; he could play for any club in the world and earn huge amounts of money. The reason that he just gets on with his job is because he's a fantastic player. I have a little chat with him now, tell him what I think. I think you get to a stage if you get so much money, you've got enough really. They don't need to become greedy. I tell Leighton, 'You're going to be rich anyway, and you're at the club that you want to be at, and playing for the club you love. Why go anywhere else?' I think it's the family ethos of a club like Everton that appeals to these players.

I don't think the board's meddling in team affairs was something we consciously talked about in the 1950s. But I think there were

times when my teammates and I were left wondering why such-and-such a player was left out or let go. You could probably surmise what was going on.

There was no advice ever given by the club on how to conduct yourself or what you should do in your own time. These days you'd be given diet sheets by nutritionists and chefs, but back then you were left to fend for yourself. I used to eat very good stuff. I love fish, and knew if you had that you would be all right. Just so long as you didn't have too much of anything.

The most I earned from playing was £20 per week at a time when my Dad was on £16. I also got £2 for a win and £1 for a draw. There was always talk of under the table payments at some clubs, but we never got any of that at Everton. The management at Goodison always played everything straight down the line. At the same time you were only ever on a one-year contract. There was no real security. If you got seriously injured you were at the mercy of the club. At the end of the season they would publish their 'Retain List' and if you weren't on it, you were finished. You had to play well to get on that list.

Dave with 8 year old fan, David Hoos of Stoneycroft, ahead of a 3-0 victory over Bolton Wanderers

There was no contract. There was also no freedom of movement, so it wasn't like you could just go and join another club.

It was, of course, a lot cheaper to go to the match back in the 1950s. Games weren't televised and there was no merchandise to speak of. Image rights? What are they? But it's not as if we had no awareness of our potential. We did all used to think, Where is the money going? I was part of Goodison's record crowd of 78,299, when they drew with Liverpool in 1948 and a few years later I would be on the other side of the barrier playing in front of 76, 74, 72,000 people.

The highest league crowd I played in front of was just short of 77,000 at Goodison against Preston in August 1954 and there were almost 78,000 when we played Manchester United there in the FA Cup a year earlier. Of course you wondered where all the gate money went. Now when you see players who are millionaires turning out in front of just 30,000 you think it's unbelievable.

Being a first-team player soon brought recognition. I was difficult to avoid because everyone knew my quiff! I quite enjoyed the attention, it was good. We had to be at Bellefield at 9.30am to start training at 10am, and my journey would be by bus to the ferry terminal, then we'd cross the Mersey by boat and get a tram to the training ground. People were great with me; you'd go to offer your sixpence fare and the ticket inspector would say, 'Put that away, Dave.' Usually I'd meet John Willie Parker on the way. We worked as a pair and we travelled as a pair. He didn't have to pay his fare either!

Training had started to develop a bit by the time I'd returned from Egypt and Britton had become manager. Typically, we'd do a warm-up, then laps of the pitch, and sometimes we'd go to Goodison and run up and down the terraces. Then came some really hard physical work, before having a game of five-a-side. We'd play different types of that game: one-touch, two-touch. Increasingly there was talk of tactics and game plans. The perception is that players back then weren't really into those sort of things, but we certainly realised how important it could be on match days.

After training they wouldn't put lunch on for us, or anything like that. We had a snooker room upstairs in the old Main Stand at Goodison and we'd sometimes make our way over there. We could have tea or coffee and hang out a bit. Mostly I just used to go straight home on public transport.

In the Goodison Main Stand was a snooker room where the players congregated after training.

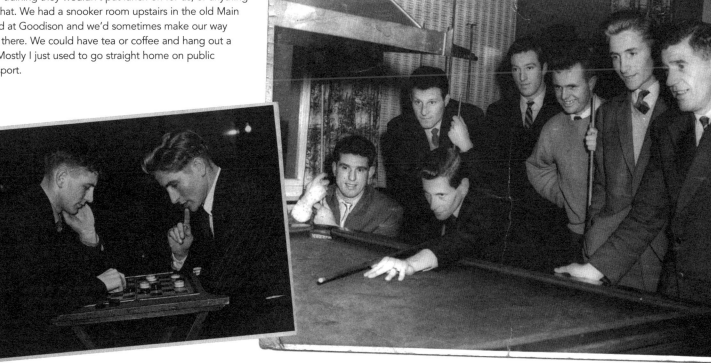

Off the pitch I didn't really socialise with any of the players. I didn't smoke or drink at the time. I was married to my first wife very young, and I used to make my way home after the game. Peter Farrell and Tommy Eglington would be the main ones who would organise the socialising among the players. I believe John Willie Parker would go out and have the odd drink now and again midweek. After Wednesdays we were told, 'Don't go drinking, that's it.' One or two used to do different things together, go to the pub or some clubs or something like that, but not me. I went home.

We used to play in old hobnail boots. You used to have to hammer them to soften them up. We'd get supplied with one pair to last us the whole season, and if they got broken you had to repair them. When you see what they play in now, it's really unbelievable. All the gear they've got is wonderful: light boots, breathable materials, a much lighter ball. I'd have loved to have played with some of that gear. Some players in the 1950s experimented with new gear. Stanley Matthews, after seeing foreign players at the 1950 World Cup, commissioned his own lightweight boots. But there was none of that for most of us. Very few players were involved in advertising or endorsements back then. If I was a player today I couldn't see myself in pink or orange boots, although there's probably money to be made from it. It's probably accepted now, but I just don't fancy the idea of wearing yellow boots or something like that!

We'd get two strips for the season. I believe the players get ten these days, but we just had to make do with the two shirts. One would get washed one week, the other the next. We had an away strip as well, but no third- or fourth-choice kits as they seem to do today.

The media attention on us was very different back then. Football wasn't really on television, except for the FA Cup final. There were radio – or wireless – broadcasts, but not like they are today. There were newspapers, of course, but it wasn't wall-to-wall coverage. But we did used to talk to the journalists after matches. I became friendly with Frank Swift, the old Manchester City goalkeeper who worked for the News of the World. He was going to write a book with me, but he died in the Munich air disaster in February 1958. I'd have to wait nearly another 60 years for the chance to tell my story.

We played in all sorts of conditions. There was no undersoil heating, so we'd play on icy or snowy pitches. It took a lot to stop a football game then. I'll always remember going to Birmingham in the Second Division. Gil Merrick, who was an England international, was in goal for Birmingham that day. We played on thick snow – I'd say there was a foot, but it had been compressed down to around six inches – but it was a great game, really exciting. We won 2–1 that day, and I scored both goals. Was it dangerous? Well, we didn't think so at the time!

Tony McNamara

FORMER EVERTON TEAM MATE

Just three weeks older than Dave Hickson, winger Tony McNamara followed him through the club's myriad reserve teams and made his debut, with Dave, during the 1951/52 season. Six years later he would take the short journey that Hickson himself would soon repeat in such controversy, and joined Liverpool. That was a short-lived move and, following spells with Crewe Alexandra and Bury during the 1957/58 season, he became the first player to appear in four different divisions in a single season.

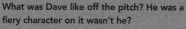

What was Dave like off the pitch? He was a fiery character on it wasn't he?
Tony McNamara: A quite different person, yes. He was very calm, didn't do anything out of place. On the pitch he was a different man altogether, he was dynamite. He put himself around, you know; charging and tackling, that sort of thing. Apart from that, a normal sort of Everton player, if there is such a thing!

Did you never see any of that sort of thing off the pitch? Did he ever lose his temper or anything?
TM: I never saw him get annoyed or anything like that, or fighting or anything.

What was he like in the dressing room?
TM: All right. It was when he got on that green place there, you know. He really moved around. And in those days of course we had five forwards so you were allowed to move from one side of the pitch to the other, whereas these days you have two playing up front so it was something different. So we had plenty of people up front and Dave would move around a lot, he'd be on the wing or at centre forward; anywhere where he could make himself felt.

Did he play like that in training as well or was it just in matches?
TM: Oh no, in training! I remember once, Bellefield was our training ground, and Harry Leyland the goalkeeper at the time. It was just two-sided, eleven-a-side and someone had a shot at goal or a pass-back or something like that. Dave went after the ball and Harry came out to pick it up. It was Harry's ball because it was near enough to him, but Dave came sliding in. Even in a practice match he was full of it. Cliff Britton the manager said, 'If you do that again you're out of this club.'

How did he react to that?
TM: Well, it's just one of those things really, a sort of rush of blood, you know. He didn't realise it was a practice match, he thought it was a game of football as far as he was concerned, he wanted to put that ball in the net; that was Dave.

Mrs McNamara: You did have a funny incident off the pitch. Pat, his wife, organised a surprise birthday party and we were all over on the Wirral at his place, all 'hush hush', until Dave walked in and we started singing 'Happy Birthday' because he was sixty. Then he said, 'I'm not, I'm only fifty-nine this year!' So we had a party then and we went back the following year for his sixtieth!

Going on from that, how did the players socialise?
TM: Well, to be honest, we didn't really see a lot of him because he was over the water at Birkenhead and we were on the Liverpool side. The only time we met each other was at away matches, say in London or wherever when you were away for a few days, then we mixed with each other and went out. But that was the only time we got together.

What did people think of him leaving? What was the reaction?
TM: I think they were a bit upset really because he was the sort of fellow that people liked because he put himself about. The spectators were probably thinking, 'He's really playing for Everton,' you know, he's doing everything; if he wants to play for the whole lot he will do, he was that sort of fellow. I think they liked him

Now it's entirely different. Pitches were not so good in those days. Nowadays the groundsman has the pitch looking like a putting green, they're absolutely fantastic, but back then we played on it in all conditions and so did the reserves.

Although Everton was a family club, we knew our place as players. The club was pretty strict when they dealt with us, not that they ever needed to discipline us much. At the time we used to have to sign a book when we went in for training. If you weren't there by 10 o'clock you were pulled up and told 'Don't do it again!' Of course, there were ways around it and the latecomers would try and sign in at five to ten if they could get away with it. It was strict and different altogether from now. Team sheets would be put up on the Friday night, and that was the team – no changing unless for a last-minute injury. It went in the papers and that was that. Now they don't

know until an hour before. The first time I started there were no substitutes allowed, but now you've got about six substitutes, so you don't know who's playing half the time; they put the lot down on Friday and you're stuck with it.

For away games we would travel by coach or train. There was no flying then! I mean, they fly down from Liverpool to Southampton now, but there was none of that, and remember these were the days before motorways too. There wouldn't normally be overnight stays either. None of us really minded. I suppose we didn't know any better. Typically we would stop off around 11.30am on the away-day journey, stretch our legs and have a light lunch – a bit of fish or something like that. On the return journey it would be straight back.

There was nothing like playing at Goodison, but I liked playing at all the big stadiums. I liked playing at Spurs, and Highbury too; they were lovely stadiums. Arsenal have got a new stadium now, haven't they? I haven't played on that yet … I suppose I might not get the chance now. Manchester City had another good stadium too.

During the summer we had loads of time off, getting on for three months in some years. There wasn't a lot to do and it was long and boring. You'd go on holiday, but our wages used to drop during the summer time as well, so that was a factor. The days were long and sometimes you'd struggle to fill them. I used to meet up with one of the Wolves players, Len Gibbons, who lived nearby and together we'd head down to the Ellesmere Port swimming baths at Overpool.

There was a lot of time to think during the summer and I'd reflect on moments in the season just gone. When you're playing during a season there are moments to reflect and sometimes it would keep me awake at night pondering what might have been (sometimes the adrenalin rush would keep me up at night as well, so lose or win there were sleepless nights) but you're thinking about the next game. During the summer there is no next game, just a long wait.

One of the things that I did was to play cricket. Dennis and Leslie Compton, the cricketing/footballing brothers of Arsenal and England, were older than me, but of my era. I was never as accomplished as them, but I played to a reasonable standard at club level on the Wirral and played a lot after I retired. As a professional footballer I played local cricket during the summer months, but not during the football season. Everton were very strict on that in case you got injured. However, they did always play an annual match at Bootle cricket club during the pre-season. I'd say I probably hit a few sixes out of Bootle Cricket Club over the years.

I'd also do a bit of training to keep ticking over because you knew that when pre-season started they were going to work you hard. Gordon Watson and Harry Cooke would have us running up and down the sand dunes in Southport, and we had a few times up in Blackpool as well. I didn't mind this at all; I couldn't get back quickly enough really. Nowadays the players have all these games in pre-season, there's not much time for all that training now. I couldn't wait.

Peter Farrell and Tommy Eglington were among a number of talented Irish players I'd play alongside during my years at Goodison. Through the 1940s and 1950s, Everton seemed to have a monopoly on Ireland's best footballers. Tommy Clinton, Jimmy O'Neill, Don Donovan and Mick Meagan all hailed from the Emerald Isle, and many fans would cross over on the ferries from Dublin to watch us play. I would have my own connection with Northern Ireland later in my career when I went to manage Ballymena.

Although I never really socialised with them, that's not to say I didn't like my teammates. I liked them all; I think that's why in the end we got promotion. You've got to have this team spirit, and I think that's what Everton have got at the moment. I like the way Everton have been the last three or four years. I think under David Moyes they had the best team and the best squad of players since Howard Kendall, which is

but they couldn't do anything about it, the club had decided to transfer him, and that was it.

Having played for Liverpool yourself as well, what was it like moving to Liverpool? Did you get any stick from fans?
Mrs M: Oh yes, well, you did in the paper…

TM: Did I? I can't remember!

Mrs M: You see I was going to get the book out last night, the scrapbook, with all these bits in.

TM: Well, I was only there sort of one season, because I'd got an injury that put me out for a few months and by the time I came back it was nearly the end of the season and they just put me on the transfer list. So I went to Crewe and went to Bury, and that was it.

So was it a big deal going to Liverpool? Was it easier than it would be now to do that?
TM: I don't know really, I didn't give it a thought. The only thing I was thinking of was 'I don't want to go to some club down South or something like that; I'd rather stay in Liverpool.' I wasn't a Liverpudlian but I'd rather play for them than go down there.

Do you think that Dave was right to leave? The way it worked out?
TM: Yes.

Mrs M: Did he have a choice?

TM: I'm sure he had a choice.

Mrs M: I don't…

TM: Well, it all depends what he was doing. If he wasn't in the game or the team, he probably thought, 'Well, I might as well have a transfer.' It was the same with me. We didn't have a manager when I got transferred, we had the directors, and what they knew about football everybody knew. So Liverpool came in for me, and I thought, 'Well, that'll do me.' I didn't have to go miles away so I thought, 'Yes, I'll go to Liverpool.' Unfortunately I got injured and at the end of the season they put me on the transfer list, it was the way it was those days.

It seems he was dropped a few times from the team and that's why he wanted to leave, but nowadays that seems a bit strange because people are dropped all the time. Is that because there were no substitutes then?
TM: Well, today there's an awful lot of money in the game, you see. If a fellow gets a good amount of money at the end of each season he doesn't want to go, he wants to stay.

Mrs M: It was the injuries in those days, wasn't it, because if they got injured and they lost their place it was really difficult and of course they used to bandage them back up to come back on again because there was no subs. Dave was a toughie, wasn't he, if you bound him up he'd come back on anyway.

TM: Well, I think there was one game against Manchester United in a cup tie which everybody talks about. And he came back on and he had a big cut, blood all over the place. That was him.

Mrs M: What was the incident when he had a referee at one time when he gave all the fouls and he stood there in the middle of the pitch saying, 'Oh, you're happy now!' Nowadays they wouldn't dare do that. If Dave was angry on the pitch then he was angry.

TM: The opposition had scored and it'd came back to the centre for kickoff and of course he was the centre forward at the kickoff and he stood there and the referee blew his whistle at him and he just stood there. He said, 'Are you happy now? You've given it to them, have you?' People would say, 'Eh, Dave, shut up.' If he did it any more the referee would say, 'I'll have to send you off, Hickson, you'd better calm down a bit,' but he was that sort of fellow.

Mrs M: They said that at the funeral, didn't they, 'You do your job and I'll do mine,' to the referee. You can just imagine that being headlines in the papers. But there was a lot of camaraderie in the game then, more than there is now. I mean all the players, they gelled and they went to places; you travelled on trains, didn't you, when you went to away games so it was all…

TM: We used to get invited to different clubs like church clubs and things like that, and of course there were a lot of people there that were Evertonians. So you used to see each other every now and again at people's clubs where they were, and that was the only time we saw each other together in midweek. But I think it was very good. They don't do that now so much because I think players now, everybody's got a beautiful big car whereas only a couple of us had a car in those days.

Jimmy Harris took Dave's place when he left. Which do you think was the better player?
TM: Oh, I'm not going to say that!

Mrs M: You'll be standing by Jimmy next week! Well, I suppose it's different really, isn't it. You can't really say who's better.

TM: I think Jimmy was probably quicker; more of a dashing player than Dave was, although Dave could put it about a bit. I think he came in when Dave got transferred.

What was the sense of expectation like among the fans? You had massive crowds all the time, but the team didn't play as well as maybe it was expected?
Mrs M: You got seventy-odd thousand, didn't you?

TM: It's only natural people were disappointed. Typical Evertonians wanted Everton to do well. I remember when we got relegated, but we were only down three years and as we came up again, Liverpool went down, and they were down for quite a long time.

Do you think Everton could have won the league in 1955 when they came back up? They seemed to be up there for a long time and then suddenly fell away…
TM: I don't know, I mean they were happy to be in the First Division, that was the thing. They probably did their best. The thing in those days was to transfer players to get a better team. We got a few players, I can't think of them all now – I'd have to have a look at a book to remember their names, pick them out!

What did you think of Cliff Britton, Ian Buchan and Johnny Carey?

TM: Well, Cliff Britton, I thought, was a good manager. I was happy for him. He always used to say, 'Get your boots on, Tone, for a rollicking.' This was when we were training. He used to come out and he was always saying, 'Tony! Tony!' And he used to say, 'Get your boots on, Tony, for a rollicking,' only in jest, like, you know. I used to like him, a good manager, better than the ones they got after that.

Cliff Britton returning to Goodison as Preston North End manager and being greeted by one of his successors, Johnny Carey.

great, and I've always admired Howard Kendall. But the way they played with Moysie is the best side I've seen for a long, long while.

Defensive players were very different in those days. You look at someone like Leighton Baines now, who goes bombing down the line for Everton and is sometimes almost like a winger. The way they play at the back now is more like a five-a-side game, with lots of interchanging. There was none of that back then, really. There was a lot of man-marking and full backs stuck to their man. Defenders defended, attackers attacked. Even at corners, despite my well-known aerial ability, I was told to hang around the halfway line in case we broke away. Of course, there were smaller players who might have been better deployed there than me, but I was the centre forward.

It's all right to say the game now is faster; it's probably faster because they've got more room now than we had. We mostly got in close to the man. We had man-markers. There wasn't space to move.

Players were also hard. Referees let a lot more go back then. Bolton were the hardest team I played against. Malcolm Barrass I've already talked about, but they had another player called Tommy Banks, who was famous for boasting that every winger who ever visited Burnden Park left with 'gravel burns'.

Cardiff's Danny Molloy was probably the hardest that I ever played against. He was no Billy Wright or John Charles, that's for sure! He was just tough, and threatening. He used to warn; 'I'll get you!' And I believed him! If Billy Wright had said that I'd have laughed. Even a hard player like Malcolm Allison wouldn't have bothered me, but I really believed Danny's threats.

Because there were no substitutes in the 1950s there were times when you had to keep on playing even when hurt or injured. You had no choice. I was never the sort of player to think, 'Bloody hell, I want to get in the bath.' The adrenalin kicked in. I never wanted a match to end.

Did Dave get on with them?
TM: [Laughs] I can imagine Dave did get on with them, off the pitch. Whether they were happy with him on the pitch I don't know! They'd say, 'You're going to get sent off, you know, just calm down, Dave.' He was that sort of fellow, cracking.

We had that spell where we had the directors in charge of the club. You used to get things passed down from the captain of the club, Peter Farrell, and a couple of the other fellows used to be asked into the directors' box when they were having their meeting in midweek.

Did you ever get to play against Dave?
TM: No, only in practice matches. Didn't really play against him because I was a forward as well, you see, and he was at the opposite end.

How do you think his style of football would fit today, in modern football?
TM: I think he'd do all right, yes. I mean, he was quick, good in the air, had a good shot; he had all the attributes of a forward. And of course he had that extra dynamite that made centre halves say, 'Get the ball away quick before he comes and gets you.' It was a bit like that.

Do you think he would have to tone it down a bit? His physical side?
TM: I don't think he could, I don't think he had it in him. When he went on the pitch, he was alive, that's what a centre forward's job is. It's also a matter of how many goals they score as well. I think at the time he got transferred, well, he might not have been getting the chances. If he wasn't scoring goals they might have thought, 'Well, let's get rid of him and have [Jimmy] Harris.'

Matt Busby told Andy Beattie, the Huddersfield manager, when he signed Hickson, that he rated him as one of the top five centre forwards in the country. How would you rate him in comparison to other players, like John Charles or Jackie Milburn?
TM: I don't know, I don't really like to pick it that way. I always took players on the actual match they were playing; he might play a blinder and the next match he might have a bad day or something. You can't really say he was great, because nobody's great all the time.

Who were the great characters at the club at the time?
TM: John Lindsay, Harry Leyland the goalkeeper, and John Willie Parker. Everybody normally when we went away to London or somewhere had a nice leather bag with all their things in. John Lindsay, the full back, he came, but he had a brown paper bag with all his things in. We said, 'Eh, Lindsay, do you realise who you're playing for? Everton Football Club.' And they picked his stuff up, opened the window and threw it out!

Interview by George Gibson

Tom Gardner

FORMER EVERTON TEAM MATE

Born in March 1923, Tom Gardner is Everton's oldest living player. With the start of his career interrupted by war, he joined Liverpool when peace came and played for the A team and reserves, before crossing Stanley Park to sign for Everton. Although he was on Everton's books for a number of years, the winger made just one appearance, during the 1947/48 season. After injury curtailed his career, he later became involved in amateur football on Merseyside. Now in his nineties, he still attends Goodison. Here he reveals his recollections of Dave Hickson as well as Everton in the 1940s and 1950s.

What was Dave Hickson like off the pitch?
Tom Gardner: Dave was a gentleman, absolute gentleman. You wouldn't have thought, to be perfectly honest, watching him on the field that you were going to get the same impression of a man off the field.

On the field, he was hard, fast, didn't care how much he got knocked about. He'd get up and get on with it. He was rough, a really, really hard centre forward.

When you got him off the field, he was so quiet, gentlemanly, one of the nicest people you could ever meet; really down to earth. Whenever you were with him, whenever you left him, he always put his hand on your arm and said, 'Okay, Tom, see you.' A smashing lad. It brings a tear to your eye when you think about him, to be honest. He was a lovely man, really lovely man.

Were you friends with him off the pitch?
TG: Not really, no, not really. Dave lived in Ellesmere Port, I live in Greasby. But when I was playing, I lived in Liverpool, so more or less when you'd finished what you were playing you went home then and obviously Dave went away. I didn't actually play with Dave, he was after me, but gave me a lot of good memories watching him; he was so good to watch. Real endeavour, he was playing to win but he was always fair, you know; he was hard but he was fair.

How did the players socialise back then?
TG: There was very, very little socialising. I'd say there was about half a dozen of us in those days. George Burnett was the reserve goalkeeper and used to have a lot of contacts. He was a great friend of the manager or the owner of a Chinese restaurant or a Far Eastern restaurant, and not every weekday but maybe once or twice a week we used to all get the bus from the ground down to Chinatown in Liverpool and we'd have a Chinese meal. There would be four or five of us; Cyril Lello, George Burnett, occasionally Peter Farrell and Tommy Eglington – [Peter and Tommy] would go down just before they got the boat back home because they lived in Ireland. I don't know how it is with the boys these days really, but we did our training, there was a snooker table we could play on and some of the boys used to stay back and some of the others used to get straight off after training and go straight home then. There was not an awful lot of socialising between the players; it was more or less come to training, do your job, enjoy your training – because we always did, we always had a lot of fun in the dressing room – and then on your way home.

What was the reaction when Dave left the club? What did fans and players think?
TG: It was sad really, sad. He was such a character. I know he was probably coming near to the end of his playing days, his main big playing days anyway, like playing for Everton. So it was sad, but on the other hand,

Everton didn't really go in for hard players until Bobby Collins arrived on the scene a few years later. However, we had some really good defenders. Jimmy Tansey and Tommy Jones had come up through the Everton ranks with me, and they were joined at the back by Don Donovan, an Irish left back. He was a fine and brave player, was Don. I always remember coming up against him when he was deputising at centre half in March 1956 and I was by then playing for Huddersfield. I scored after just 45 seconds and had a really good game against him. But he was a fine player and never let anyone down.

At Goodison we always had good goalkeepers. Ted Sagar was at the end of his career, but a great keeper – one of the best Everton have ever had and the best I ever played with. I think Jimmy O'Neill was a really good keeper. Harry Leyland was in the reserves and played a bit in the first team before he went to Blackburn. But Ted was the one.

Ted had made his first Everton appearance when I was just three months old, and I ended up playing in Ted's last ever game nearly 24 years later. There were lots of good keepers at the time though: Gil Merrick at Birmingham, Arsenal had a good keeper in Jack Kelsey, and Charlton had Sam Bartram, who was fantastic.

I never used to fear anyone. No opponent concerned me, but I respected them, particularly the goalkeepers – who were very brave. Manchester City's goalkeeper Bert Trautmann was a very good keeper. He'd been a German prisoner of war and had settled in the north-west afterwards and played for Manchester City, famously playing on in the FA Cup final after breaking his neck. He was my type of player!

Dave's 1955 move to Aston Villa was front page news in Birmingham.

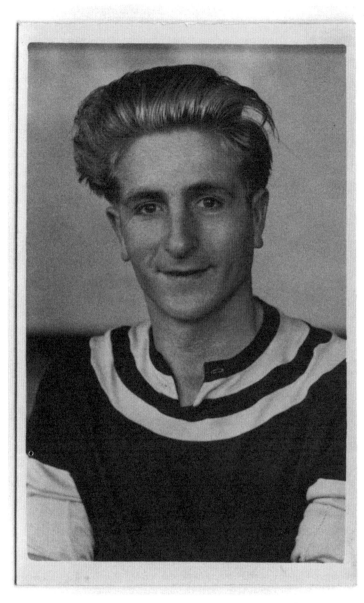

There were a couple of sides to my public image, neither of which were completely accurate. On the one hand I had a reputation as a blond, Boy's Own-type hero, on the front of football magazines. People saw me as a hero or iconic figure. On the other I was a bit of a controversial player; a bruiser, a hard man.

Which one of these was the real Dave Hickson? I suppose I was a bit of both, although I never considered myself a hero. I gave everything I had, that's all I can say. I played as well as I could for all my clubs. It was my fellow Portite, Joe Mercer, who asked the question which prompted my most famous quote. Joe said to me, 'How are you liking Everton, Dave? How are you liking it, son?'

I replied, 'Put it this way, Joe, I'd break every bone in my body for any club I played for, but I'd die for Everton.'

I said it to Joe and everyone picked up on it. I said it because I loved the place, always did and always will. They treated me great. When I had my heart attack in 2007 they did everything they could to look after me. Even now, at 83 years of age, I'm still on their books. They mean everything to me. They're a great club.

you know, life moves on and you miss Dave anyway. I wasn't at the club when Dave was playing, I was only a spectator really watching him.

GG: So what did you think of him moving to Liverpool? Did he get a lot of stick from fans then?
TG: When I went to Liverpool I was in Liverpool reserves. I played for Liverpool A team, and then I played for Liverpool's reserve side and I enjoyed my time at Liverpool but deep down I'm an Evertonian. When I got the opportunity to cross the park, I came here and was made very welcome. They took me down to the dressing room, introduced me to every player who was in the dressing room and got a lovely handshake off them. Everything was friendly and it was exactly as I thought about Everton Football Club. As a boy I used to go to Liverpool and I used to go to Everton. I had an uncle who used to take me every week, as my father died when I was very young, I was only seven because he was gassed in the First World War. So of course it was my uncle who used to come to football and he'd take me to Liverpool one week and Everton the next week.

So whereas I am deep-down Blue, I still think a lot of Liverpool anyway. I enjoyed my time there, I made a lot of friends there at Liverpool, and in fact one of my deepest, best friends was Bill Liddell, who was one of my idols as well, even though I was an Evertonian. Bill was such a good player. Then years later, when I finished football, I took up a coaching course and I'd come to the Merseyside Youth Representative team for twenty years, and Bill Liddell was their chairman so I got to know him very, very well and became very friendly with Bill. I had no reaction from the Everton players at all for crossing the park, they never pulled my leg, they never said anything about it, just accepted me because I think at that time they knew I was an Evertonian anyway – I didn't need to tell them because I could talk Everton, let's put it that way.

Do you think Dave was right to leave?
TG: No, I don't think he was right to leave Everton. I don't think anybody is right to leave Everton!

I think he was upset at being dropped a few times...
TG: That was what it was, that was why. He did tell me one time that he'd had a few words at being dropped. He let them know that he wasn't happy about it and I think at that time he'd made his mind up that he wanted away, and he did and that was it. It was a shame really because he had such a loyalty to Everton. I think he made a mistake really, going to Liverpool. He was purely and simply an Everton man, like myself, and I do honestly think he made a mistake going, but there we are.

It seems strange for him to drop down a division as well, and then when he left Liverpool he went into non-league. It seems like quite a big step when he seems to have had offers to stay in the top division instead?
TG: I don't know what it was with Dave. With Dave Hickson he never thought he was a star or anything like that; he never had that ambition to be the top man. He was Dave Hickson and he was an Everton footballer or he was a footballer but he was never big-headed. He was more subdued, that was his make-up. I think the other thing was that if an opportunity arose for whatever reason he would accept it, he would take it. He was easy-going and yet he was a bit of a worrier as well over little things, whether it was family or whatever, I don't know.

Do you think it's maybe wanting to feel wanted?
TG: Yeah, I think you've probably hit the nail on the head because he was that kind of man. He wanted to be liked – and he was liked – but he wanted to be wanted as well. That was his make-up.

After he left, Jimmy Harris replaced him in the side. Who do you think was the better player for Everton?
TG: Dave Hickson.

No doubt?
TG: No doubt, but Jimmy was a good player, don't misunderstand me. And again, Jimmy's a nice man, a nice bloke, a very nice bloke. Dave Hickson, no argument.

So do you think Everton made a mistake there?
TG: Yes, no argument!

What was the sense of expectation like among the fans? Because there were often big crowds, but the team didn't really do as well as possibly it was hoped...TG: I think the expectation was 'Who's this fellow that's going to take over from Dave?' kind of thing. Everybody had that same feeling that nobody is going to be as good as Dave Hickson. So he came in under a cloud, really, although people were expecting big things, he did come in under a cloud and I think that was the loss of Dave.

Do you think that during the early 1950s and onwards, the club really under-achieved? It was in the Second Division for quite a while and then when it came back up they looked like they were possibly going to win the league in the first season back, and then filtered off at the end of the season. Why do you think that happened?
TG: I don't know, they had all the same players, and they'd made one or two signings but football is football: you can have a good game one week and then for some reason or another you can fall down the next week, and I think it was a bit that way really in that there was no actual feeling of everybody not doing their job, not working hard, not doing their best. I think it's football, it's just one of those things like life, isn't it? Life has ups and downs, football has its ups and downs.

What did you think of the managers around that time?
TG: The manager when I was at Everton was Theo Kelly, and to be perfectly honest he was getting a bit past-it. He spent most of his time in the office, you never saw very much of him on the field. Like the managers these days, take the likes of David Moyes; he's out on the field with the boys, he's completely embroiled with them if you like, like all the managers now these days. Theo Kelly was in his office, and you never saw him come out onto the field, I don't think he knew what football was about, to be honest.

Cliff Britton was a different kettle of fish. He'd been a good footballer, Cliff, a wonderful footballer, and he knew his football. I felt he was a bit hard. Now whether we weren't used to that kind of thing I don't know, but he was an 'I'm the boss,' put your thumb on it, 'I'm the boss and you'll do as I tell you' type of thing, and very strong. A bit like Shankly really, although Shankly did have a nice way with him as well. Cliff Britton was a bit off-handed, not exactly abusive, but he was the boss.

Do you think that's a good thing?
TG: To a point, only to a point. I think David Moyes was a boss. I think the manager has got to be somebody who says, 'I am the boss, you will do as I tell you,' but in a nice way, not lay down the law and say, 'This is it,' like swings and roundabouts. I think Cliff was a bit harsh really and I wasn't with him all that very long but I think he was a bit harsh. Jock Thomson came in for a short while after Theo Kelly finished as a coach. Now he was a different man, a Scots lad, been a good footballer, got on well with the boys, one of those that explained things, what he wanted and all the rest of it, whereas Cliff was 'You will do what I tell you' sort of thing, 'Do this, do that,' and if you didn't do it you were in trouble.

Do you think maybe he would have clashed with Dave Hickson, and that's why Dave was upset?
TG: Dave was one of those chaps you could shout at him, scream at him, tell him anything you wanted, which happened on the field occasionally in training because I've seen this happen and I've heard stories and Dave has told me as well. Dave would accept it, 'That's it, that's it,' never argued. I think towards the end of his career, you know when you've had enough of something, I felt with Dave he'd had enough, he was getting to the end and he'd had enough, he wanted out.

I always got on all right at the club, until the start of the 1955/56 season when Cliff Britton left me out without saying why. What's worse, he didn't even play me in the reserves. I'd been doing all right. Myself and John Willie had scored 31 goals between us the previous season. I spent a lot of time thinking 'why?' He never told me, so I was left to wonder for myself. Was it my discipline? At the time Everton were very, very strict on that. They wouldn't have anyone who was booked all the time, sent off or anything like that. That was pretty much unheard of in those days. I did get on the wrong side of referees and I'm not proud of it. I only got sent off three times in my career, and two of them were speaking back to the referee; the other one was for a tackle on a player at the Kop while I was at Liverpool.

We were 3–0 up at the time against Sheffield United. They had two Shaws playing for them – Graham and Joe – and one of them tackled me. It was a bad tackle and I chased him down to the Kop end and slid him into touch, ball and man. I was sent off. Bill Shankly protected me on that one. I went to tribunal with Jimmy Hill, who was in charge of the players union, and got off on that one.

The other two dismissals, as I say, were for speaking to the referee. One was at Maine Road in December 1957 when we got beaten 6–2. Ken Barnes scored a hat-trick of penalties and Billy McAdams scored a brace of offside goals. I wasn't happy at all, so I went to the referee.

'Do you realise what you're doing here?' I said. I was animated, but I wasn't swearing. 'I'm not kicking off here, but do you realise what you've done? You've given three penalties and two offside goals.'

The referee just looked at me blankly.

'I'm not playing you,' he said. 'Get off.' And he sent me off.

I never swore when I was on the pitch. I might have said 'bloody' every now and then, but nothing bad. The Everton management were all right then, but I felt that under Britton maybe

Within months of joining Aston Villa Dave was on the move again, this time to Huddersfield Town.

What do you think about the style of football though? Do you think, for example, Dave Hickson would have fitted into the modern game?

TG: I don't think Dave would have fitted in at all. When we played it was direct, maybe I'm giving it the wrong way, but I felt it was direct football. You had two full backs, three half backs, five forwards; that was attacking, and all teams played the same thing, there was no difference. It was only later that the 4–3–3, 4–2–4 came in. Those days you were told point-blank to get the ball forward, get it forward all the time. The wingers, for instance, where I was playing, we weren't full backs, we were at the halfway line and forward, don't go back; the two full backs looked after their forwards, the three half backs looked after their inside forwards and the wingers were wingers and you stayed on that wing.

In those days, if you see the old photographs, the wingers were always halfway down the pitch. They always used to tell us as well, 'Don't pass the ball back unless you've got to.' It's fatal. Now, in this game, the ball is being passed back and forwards and back and back and back. Pretty, clever; brilliant passers of the ball, some of these lads now, but ours was direct; down the wing, slash it across, full whack to the centre forward; that's why Hickson did so well. The ball was down the wing and over to him and bunk, he'd go in, you know. Tommy Lawton, Dixie Dean were exactly the same.

Do you think it was more exciting then like that?

TG: Yes, it was exciting. It was, definitely. I mean, to see Bill Liddell go down that left wing it was absolutely magic. It really was magic. And we had them: Tommy Eglington, left-winger; he would be down that wing like a shot. Peter was his mate, Peter Farrell at left half, and Peter and Tommy were good. Tommy seemed to know what Pete was going to do with that ball, knew exactly where it was going to go. It was good, it was fast, it was good football. Not the speed that we've got today, but more direct. There was very little of the back-passing; you see the old films and there was very little, they did do the odd back-pass but we were told – [the trainer] Harry Cooke used to say, 'Don't pass the ball back unless you've got to!' And you wouldn't. The full back would get in trouble if he was back-passing because the wingers were so quick. I was quick as well. And if the ball was passed back you would be in like a shot, and with the two full backs you could get the ball in between the two of them more than when you've got four full backs now.

So it was a very attacking game?

TG: Very attacking game, yes, very attacking. It was good to watch, good football, it was exciting and you knew you were going to get four or five goals whereas now it's one goal and win.

So do you think someone like Dave Hickson was very much a man of his time?
TG: Definitely.

Suited that style of play?
TG: Definitely suited that type of play.

Whereas now he might not be as effective? Not as many balls into the box...
TG: Dave would be one of those lads I think who'd be frustrated now with this kind of football. Most centre forwards, I don't know, you can talk about Suarez if you like; good footballer, not a centre forward, but a good footballer and he's good up front and he can dribble and takes goals just like that, very, very clever. But I don't think to be perfectly honest he would have been suitable for the type of football that we played in those days. Different, completely different type of football.

Interview by George Gibson

Dated   23rd November,   1955.

THE

HUDDERSFIELD TOWN

Football Club

AND

DAVID HICKSON

AGREEMENT
FOR HIRE OF A PLAYER

An Agreement made the 23rd

day of November, 19 55. between Harry

Beever of Leeds Road,

Huddersfield in the COUNTY OF Yorkshire.

the Secretary of and acting pursuant to Resolution and Authority for and on

behalf of the Huddersfield Town FOOTBALL CLUB

of Leeds Road, Huddersfield. (hereinafter referred to as the Club)

of the one part and David Hickson

of Pond House, 315 Wakefield Road, Huddersfield.

in the COUNTY OF Yorkshire. Professional Football Player

(hereinafter referred to as the Player) of the other part **Whereby** it is agreed
as follows:—

1. The Player hereby agrees to play in an efficient manner and to the best
of his ability for the Club.

2. The Player shall attend the Club's ground or any other place decided
upon by the Club for the purposes of or in connection with his training as a
Player pursuant to the instructions of the Secretary, Manager, or Trainer of the
Club, or of such other person, or persons, as the Club may appoint. (This
provision shall not apply if the Player is engaged by the Club at a weekly wage
of less than One Pound, or at a wage per match.)

3. The Player shall do everything necessary to get and keep himself in the
best possible condition so as to render the most efficient service to the Club, and
will carry out all the training and other instructions of the Club through its
representative officials.

4. The Player shall observe and be subject to all the Rules, Regulations
and Bye-Laws of The Football Association, and any other Association, League,
or Combination of which the Club shall be a member. And this Agreement shall
be subject to any action which shall be taken by The Football Association under
their Rules for the suspension or termination of the Football Season, and if any
such suspension or termination shall be decided upon the payment of wages shall
likewise be suspended or terminated, as the case may be.

5. The Player shall not engage in any business or live in any place which
the Directors (or Committee) of the Club may deem unsuitable.

6. If the Player shall be guilty of serious misconduct or breach of the
disciplinary Rules of the Club, the Club may, on giving 14 days' notice
to the said Player, or the Club may, on giving 28 days' notice to the said Player,
on any reasonable grounds, terminate this Agreement and dispense with the
services of the Player (without prejudice to the Club's right for transfer fees)
in pursuance of the Rules of all such Associations, Leagues, and Combinations
of which the Club may be a member. Such notice or notices shall be in writing,
and shall specify the reason for the same being given, and shall also set forth the
rights of appeal to which the Player is entitled under the Rules of The Football
Association.

The Rights of Appeal are as follows:—

Any League or other Combination of Clubs may, subject to these Rules, make such regulations
between their Clubs and Players as they may deem necessary. Where Leagues and Combinations
are sanctioned direct by this Association an Appeals Committee shall be appointed by this Association.
Where Leagues and Combinations are sanctioned by County Associations an Appeals Committee
shall be appointed by the sanctioning County Associations. Where an agreement between a Club
and a Player in any League or other Combination provides for the Club terminating by notice to
the Player of the Agreement between the Club and Player on any reasonable ground the following
practice shall prevail: A Player shall have the right of appeal to the Management Committee of
his League or Combination and a further right of appeal to the Appeals Committee of that body.
A Club on giving notice to a Player to terminate his Agreement must state in the notice the name
and address of the Secretary of the League or Combination to which he may appeal, and must also
at the same time give notice to the League or Combination of which the Club is a member. A copy
of the notice sent to the Player must at the same time be forwarded to the Secretary of this Association.
The Player shall have the right of appeal to the League or Combination, but such appeal must be
made within 7 days of the receipt of the Notice from the Club. The Notice terminating the Agreement
must inform the Player the reasons or grounds for such Notice. The appeal shall be heard by the
Management Committee within 10 days of the receipt of the Notice from the Player. If either
party is dissatisfied with the decision, there shall be a right of further appeal to the Appeals Committee
of the League or Combination, but such appeal must be made within 7 days of the receipt of the
intimation of the decision of the Management Committee, and must be heard by the Appeals Committee within 10 days of the receipt of the Notice of Appeal. The League or Combination shall
report to this Association when the matter is finally determined, and the Agreement and Registration
shall be cancelled by this Association where necessary. Agreements between Clubs and Players
shall contain a clause showing the provision made for dealing with such disputes and for the cancelling
of the Agreements and Registrations by this Association. Clubs not belonging to any League or
Combination before referred to may, upon obtaining the approval of this Association, make similar
regulations. Such regulations to provide for a right of appeal by either party to the County Association, or to this Association.

7. This Agreement and the terms and conditions thereof shall be as to its
suspension and termination subject to the Rules of The Football Association and
to any action which may be taken by the Council of The Football Association or
any deputed Committee, and in any proceedings by the Player against the Club
it shall be a sufficient and complete defence and answer by and on the part of
the Club that such suspension or termination hereof is due to the action of The
Football Association, or any Sub-Committee thereof to whom the power may be
delegated.

8. Notwithstanding anything contained in the Rules of The Football
Association, the registration of the player shall remain in force in the event of the
player being called for Military Service, and shall remain effective until the end
of the season in which the player is demobilised, unless determined at an earlier
date by mutual agreement between the Club and the player.

9. In consideration of the observance by the said player of the terms,

provisions and conditions of this Agreement, the said Harry

Beever on behalf of the Club hereby agrees that the said

Club shall pay to the said Player the sum of £14. 0. 0. per week from

23rd November, 1955. to 5th May, 1956.

and £ 12. 0. 0. per week from 7th May, 1956.

to 30th June, 1956.

10. This Agreement (subject to the Rules of The Football Association)

shall cease and determine on 30th June, 1956.

unless the same shall have been previously determined in accordance with the

provisions hereinbefore set forth.

(1) It is hereby agreed by the player that if he shall at any time first team.
during such absence, be entitled to receive only the difference
between his full weekly wages, and the amount he receives as
benefit under the National Insurance Act 1946 or the National
Insurance (Industrial Injuries) Act, 1946 and for the purpose of
this clause his wages shall be deemed to accrue from day to day.

(2) If at any time during the period of this Agreement the wages
herein agreed to be paid shall be in excess of the wages permitted
to be paid by the Club to the player in accordance with the Rules
of the Football League, the wages to be paid to the player shall be
the amount the Club is entitled to pay by League Rules in force
from time to time and this Agreement shall be read and construed
as if it were varied accordingly.

As witness the hands of the said parties the day and year first aforesaid

Signed by the said Harry

Beever and David

Hickson

In the presence of

(Signature) _J. Galvin_

(Occupation) Assistant Secretary

(Address) 6 Ryefields Avenue,

Quarmby, Huddersfield.

D. Hickson (Player)

Harry Beever (Secretary)

Harry Ross

FORMER VICAR OF ST LUKE THE EVANGELIST

The Reverend Harry Ross was vicar of St Luke the Evangelist, next door to Goodison Park, for more than three decades as well as a key figure in the Everton Former Players Foundation, through which he befriended Dave.

I began to see Dave at Goodison on a regular basis when he was taking people around the ground on tours, and I had the church at the corner. We developed a friendship. I knew his wife Pat and got to know her very well, and I got to know him much better when the Everton Former Players Foundation began and he was having one or two difficulties health-wise and we helped him and gave him some assistance.

Our relationship really got stronger when he suffered a heart attack before a match against Sunderland in November 2007 and I went up to the hospital with him. He had had a very severe heart attack and the doctors were looking after him and giving him all kinds of treatment. I was telling him about the game – we were winning at that time 4–0 or something like that – and he prevailed on me to go back and ask Bill Kenwright if he could still have his job at Goodison when he came back.

I tried to reassure him that there would be no problem with that, but in order to make sure he didn't get any worse I had to come all the way back from the Royal Hospital to Goodison to go and see Bill, get the assurance - which I knew already – and get back up to the hospital to reassure Dave, by which time we've beaten them 7–1.

From there on our friendship grew very, very strong and I went over to his house on several occasions to meet with him and Pat. Of course, his health began to deteriorate in different ways. He had all kinds of things starting to happen and we all gave him help in practical ways as well as in medical ways. Later, I officiated when his wife's funeral took place.

One occasion that does keep coming back is his eightieth birthday. We arranged a party for him in what was the marquee at Goodison, but he thought it was only going to be just a few friends and a small informal gathering. What he didn't know was it was an absolutely full marquee. However, we thought we'd have to call it off because he was so ill. On the day of the party he signed himself out of the hospital and we arranged for him to be brought by a car from the hospital to the marquee, where we got a wheelchair for him. However, Dave was adamant that he wouldn't go in a wheelchair from the car to the top of the ramp because everybody could see. He

that counted against me. When he left me out I was done with him. It set me back a lot. He'd told me I'd play for England. It was a big letdown being left out and I didn't want to be unwanted, so when a couple of clubs came in for me I told Everton I wanted to leave.

Indeed, my discipline might have cost me England recognition as well. I came close a few times to getting called up, but England had a great centre forward in Nat Lofthouse, and also Manchester United's Tommy Taylor. Both Cliff Britton and Johnny Carey told me I was good enough to play for my country, but the call-up never came. I was told that the England manager at the time, Walter Winterbottom, didn't like that kind of thing at all. He didn't like anyone who'd been booked in his team!

'I want to get away from Everton now the die is cast and make a fresh start elsewhere,' I told reporters. 'I am only 25 and I feel that I have got good football in me, yet somehow I have come to the conclusion that I shall not reproduce it at Everton.'

I didn't really want to go, of course. My problem was that I was too much in love with the game. I wanted to be out there playing all the time.

Aston Villa were one of the clubs that came in and promised they'd play me all the time. I didn't want to go at all, but I desperately wanted to play football and be somewhere that I was wanted. That's all I wanted to do. It wasn't about money – you got the same wherever you went. I wanted to play football every week. My fee was £19,500. It was big money back then [the transfer record was £35,000] and it probably played on my mind a little bit. There was no signing-on fee, however, nothing at all like that. I was only there a few months and scored just the one goal, against Manchester United. I did all right at Villa, there were some good players.

I didn't really want to want to move house or leave the area where I'd grown up and spent my life, so I was living in a hotel in Birmingham and stayed in my room all the time. It wasn't ideal, but at least I was playing.

My forward partner was the Northern Ireland international winger Peter McParland, who was a really good player. We struggled a bit in the league, however, and at the end Villa only avoided relegation on goal average.

By then I'd moved on to Huddersfield Town, after being signed by Andy Beattie for £16,500 just four months into my stay at Villa Park. Because Villa had been struggling there was still a feeling that they needed to change things around. They opted to go for Sheffield Wednesday's Jackie Sewell, but needed to fund the deal and so made the decision to sell me. I was fine with the move; Huddersfield were in the top flight and a good side.

Andy Beattie made me realise that my old impetuosity was not a good thing. He impressed on me that I could be just as good a player, and possibly a better one, if I would use my intelligence a little more. Whenever he thought I was acting first and thinking afterwards he took me aside and lectured me.

I'd been bought to partner Jimmy Glazzard in attack, who was the club's record goalscorer. Unfortunately he was injured and our partnership was never properly tested. I scored nine goals during the rest of the 1955/56 season, but it wasn't enough. We lost out to Villa on goal average and dropped out of the top flight. However, we were very, very unlucky. Villa started the final day of the season hoping to win at home against West Bromwich Albion to give them the best chance of staying up, but we were a point ahead of them and in control of our own destiny. Villa could only draw with West Brom, but we were unable to stave off a 4–1 defeat to Burnley. It was a disaster. We finished level on points, but went down on goal average. Everton finished five points clear of the drop zone.

Andy had recently managed Scotland at the World Cup, but after relegation he was dismissed by the Huddersfield board. Jimmy Glazzard left, ironically, for Goodison, where he played just three games before moving on to Mansfield Town. Andy's assistant, who had played with him at Preston North End, was appointed in his place. His name is now familiar to anyone with any knowledge of English football and would have a significant bearing on my career: Bill Shankly.

We had a good young team at Huddersfield and I look back on my time there with happiness. Despite going down, it was, for me, a wonderful couple of years. I scored goals and my partner up front was a 16-year-old Scottish prodigy by the name of Denis Law. When he was first brought down to Yorkshire, Andy Beattie famously said: 'The boy's a freak. Never did I see a less likely football prospect – weak, puny and bespectacled.' It was a view with which I agreed: he didn't look as if he could play at all, and wore these NHS glasses, but by heck was he a fine player. He was only a young boy, but when he was on the pitch you could tell he was a good player, that he was going to make it. We got on well too, which always helps.

Ray Wilson was there as well. He wasn't very old, but he came in the team and did a good job. You could see that he was going to make it to the top. We had a winger called Vic Metcalfe, who had played for England. He provided many crosses for the goals that I scored.

I started the 1956/57 season playing some of the best football of

was that proud. But he was glad he made it; when he walked in and saw how many people had come, you could see the tears in his eyes. There were many, many people, from Everton and different clubs he'd played at, including all his friends in show business, because he was very popular. At the end of it we managed to smuggle him back into his wheelchair again and out into the car.

Dave loved being at Goodison. He loved all the associations and memories Goodison had for him, all of the friends that he had. One of the jobs he really enjoyed was showing people around the ground, into the dressing rooms, taking them on tours. On match days he thoroughly enjoyed going into the sponsors' lounge, going around to the team, talking to people, going on the pitch. He loved Goodison so much and he didn't want to miss that. There were many occasions when he wasn't really well enough to go around and we tried to prevail on him just to sit in the lounge and watch the game in comfort. But he wanted to be among people. He loved being among Evertonians and wanted to be with them. That was his home.

It was the same stubborn brave streak that had defined him as a player. It was part of his character. He never gave up. There were times when Everton would say to me, 'Please ask him just to sit there and get people to come to him,' but no, Dave was not that kind of man. If he had a job to do he did it to the best of his ability, even if he wasn't strong enough, well enough.

I think it was his single-mindedness for Everton, his dedication to anything and everything for Everton that made him so unique, so well loved. I have seen him over the years, when he was playing, blood streaming off his head, still going. I think today he probably would have been given the red card because of some of the tackles he used to do. Off the field he was a gentleman, on the field an absolute terrier.

There were other popular players, but they knew that there were other teams and other things going on. But he was single-minded over Everton, they were so important to him. He loved it when Pat was by his side, enjoying the same things. Goodison was his home, he loved it. I think it was his single-mindedness in his passion for Everton and what Everton stood for that made him so popular. Although he played for other teams, nothing came up to the standard as far as he was concerned. He would do anything for Everton, you would get everything from him.

I think that's why Bill Kenwright was drawn to him, because of his passion for Everton and everything to do with it. He and Bill really enjoyed a wonderful relationship, almost like a father and son. Bill had so much admiration for Dave. He had been his idol from the very beginning and everything Bill enjoyed about football was embodied in Dave. Bill invited Dave on many occasions down to London and other places and formed a great bond. I know that Dave loved Bill very much indeed. I think he realised Bill was unique, because he isn't just a chairman, he is an Evertonian, and loves the Blues as much as Dave did. That's the passion that they shared and Dave looked up to Bill and Bill looked up to Dave. Bill really grieved when Dave left this earth.

I don't think we'll see anyone of his like again. The modern game isn't the same. To see the passion in Dave on the field was something else. Today you can't breathe on opponents, but Dave would take them apart. He wasn't paid a lot of money, but he was so passionate about football.

my career. I scored 15 goals in my first 19 matches and, with a bit of luck, I might have had an even better return. Then I got an ankle injury which knocked me off my perch and had to spend some time in the second team trying to get fit. We finished the season in a disappointing twelfth position.

I was mostly happy at Leeds Road, but football can take unexpected twists. Lo and behold, in the summer of 1957 Everton came back for me. The fee, £6,500 – a third of what they'd sold me for. As much as I liked Huddersfield, I couldn't get back quickly enough.

The transfer dragged on for a number of weeks. While the newspapers filled with speculation about my destiny – Tranmere Rovers, West Ham, Chesterfield and Stockport were all reported to be interested – there was only one place for me.

The letters pages of the *Liverpool Echo* filled up with fans imploring the club to seal the deal. E. Lowe of Corsewell Street, Liverpool 7, wrote: 'Hickson was Everton's biggest attraction since Dixie Dean. The gates will jump if he comes here again. I say: sign him. The crowd want Dave back again.' S.T. Quayle of Anfield added: 'I was dreading the coming football season until the news that Everton had made a bid for Hickson.'

No one wanted to be there more than me. When the transfer went through it was a great homecoming at Everton. I really enjoyed it, but then how could you not? They were my club. It was the happiest day of my life when I returned to Goodison.

'I cannot tell you how glad I am to be an Everton player again,' I told reporters. 'I never really wanted to leave, and have never been happy since I did. It feels grand to be back and I mean to do my utmost to play better in the future than I ever did in the past.'

In an article for the *Liverpool Echo*, I expanded upon my delight:

The past week has been one of the happiest of my life.

Today I am older and – I hope – wiser, and though my delight at again being an Evertonian has been deep and profound, there has been more to it than that. I have learned a lot in the two years I have been away from Goodison Park. I realise that more is expected from me than ever before, and that it is up to me to do my utmost to see that neither the directors of the club nor its supporters are disappointed.

If hard and earnest endeavour will enable me to justify that faith then you will not find me wanting. Never before in my life have I been so anxious to make good; not for my own sake, but for the sake of the finest club in the country and the many supporters who were in favour of my return to Goodison Park.

It was due to a misunderstanding that I left Goodison. I have since regretted it almost from the very first day. It is not for me to try to apportion blame. I don't even want to seem to be making excuses for myself.

I know this, however. If I had my time to come over again I should act in a very different manner. In short, I have learned by experience and hope that as a consequence I shall be a better servant of the Everton club in the future than I was in the past.

Maybe I acted a little hastily. But if those who have never done the same throughout their lives refrain from casting stones, and only the blameless do so, I shall not complain.

65, Liverpool Road,
Penwortham,
Preston.
4th Sept. 1957.

Dear Davie,

I am delighted with the start you have made with your old club. I follow most of the old players, and I like to think they do well. I have been very interested in you and the reports so far are very good. The press are really with you so you can make it from now on providing you remember to stop breathing, count ten, and then the heat will have worn off.

I had the article forwarded on to me that you wrote in the local press. It was very nice Davie, - thank you.

I felt I always did my best for all the players even if at times they did not always appreciate it.

Anyway, I will be following you, so all the very best and try hard to make the other clubs realise how good a player they really lost. Not that I wish any of them harm, I only wish you well.

Best wishes.
Sincerely,

Andy Beattie

Mike Hughes

BBC RADIO MERSEYSIDE

I never had the privilege of seeing Dave Hickson in action in 'real life', apart from the odd short clip of newsreel footage, but that certainly doesn't diminish his status as one Merseyside's football legends.

To listen to and read the descriptions of his all-round talents highlights what an incredible footballer he was. The fact that he's held in such high esteem right across the Merseyside football divide is further evidence of a very special player. His undoubted ability was allied to a will to win, that underlined his desire to not only do well for his team, but to serve the paying public.

He was a very special man. I got to know him very well when he returned to Everton as a club ambassador in the mid-1990s. I interviewed him on scores of occasions and his eyes would light up whenever he recalled bygone days and his particular passion for Everton.

His place among the legendary Everton number nines is fully justified. He was a wonderfully entertaining character and one of life's real gentlemen.

Gone, but never ever forgotten.

Ian Buchan had taken over from Cliff Britton as manager during my two years away. He'd been a university PT instructor and an amateur player in Scotland. He was very strict indeed as a coach. I don't know how much influence he had on team selection – I think that the board still had a lot of say in those days. Now the manager manages, the chairman leaves everything to him, but will help out and support him on some things. You look at how David Moyes worked with Bill Kenwright and that's something that worked very well. But back then we were never really sure who had the final say.

Results didn't go Ian's way, but I liked him and thought that he was a good manager. A lot has been made of his background as a sports lecturer, but I don't remember anything different on the training ground. It was mostly the same as it always had been; lots of lapping, head tennis, five-a-sides. At Everton we were brought up to play good football. I liked to get stuck in, but playing attractive football was very important too. There was only so much anybody could ever teach us.

Although I was number nine, there was competition for my place. Ian Buchan brought in new signings in an attempt to redress Everton's decline. Jimmy Harris, who usually played as inside forward, was sometimes tried in my place and Alec Ashworth and Peter Harburn were brought in, tried and discarded. As you can probably tell by now, I didn't like not playing.

Manchester United were a great side during this era. They won the league early in the decade, with the experienced Johnny Carey the key man and players like Jack Rowley. Then Matt Busby rebuilt the side around youth – players he had scouted or developed himself – and they were a cracking team, winning back-to-back titles. They had a brilliant young forward called Bobby Charlton and their centre forward, Tommy Taylor, was a super player too. The star and lynchpin was Duncan Edwards, a real Rolls-Royce type of player. You could see he was destined to be one of the greats.

Four games into my second coming at Everton we played them at Goodison. There were nearly 72,000 people there and it was a fantastic game, finishing 3–3. I remember heading a couple of balls on for Derek Temple, who was a promising young winger starting out, to score – similar to how he'd later score in the 1966 FA Cup final … a flick-on and Derek would break clear and crash them in. I think that helped make Derek. He was really on the way after that.

So many of my best moments in an Everton shirt came against Manchester United – the FA Cup tie, beating them 4–2 a couple of months after returning to the top flight, that whirlwind draw. But the 3–3 game would be a watershed encounter, the last time I'd compete against many of those players. Five months later we couldn't believe it when we heard what had happened, that they had died in an air accident in Munich. We just couldn't believe something like that had happened. Tommy Taylor, Duncan Edwards and six other United players were among the 23 dead. They included my mate Frank Swift, the former Man City goalkeeper turned News of the World journalist who was going to help me write a book.

Everton finished the 1957/58 campaign sixteenth, a place down on the previous season, and exited the FA Cup in the fourth round. It was a time of transition. Peter Farrell and Tommy Eglington had joined Tranmere

Rovers, Jackie Grant had gone to Rochdale, and Don Donavon moved to Grimsby Town. Wally Fielding began to be edged out. Meanwhile a new generation of players began to be introduced to the first team: as well as Derek Temple and Jimmy Harris, there were the two Brians: Labone and Harris.

I'll always remember playing against Brian Labone for the first time. It was a few weeks after my return to Goodison, in the Blues v. Whites match, which they used to have them at the beginning of the season. Brian was 17 and only a month out of school. Now they go all over the world for their pre-season matches, but this was a big thing at the time and you used to get a lot of people going along. And Brian Labone was a young lad in the second team at the time and he played centre half against me. You could see straight away that he was going to make it, he was so steady and cool. He reminded me of John Charles, who was a fantastic centre half as well as a great centre forward; he was probably one of the best I ever played against really. Brian's positional play was good, like Charles's; he was very very hard to break down. He had me baffled, to be honest.

There were some defenders that had a certain thing about them; they just knew the game and you had to pit your wits against them. Brian and John Charles were those sort of players. Then there were those who'd go head to head with you. They'd do you. Hurt you. I didn't mind who I was playing against – I just wanted to play.

Brian Harris was a good wing half. He came into the team when I was playing and, like Brian Labone, went on to play a very important role when Everton won the FA Cup in 1966.

The man who won the FA Cup that day for Everton was Derek Temple. He was just a kid making his name for himself in the 1950s and then had his career interrupted by national service. Like me a decade earlier he thought that halted his career progress a bit, but he recovered and became a key part of the Everton team in the 1960s. Some people said he wasn't that fast, but once he got into his stride there was no stopping him. His finest moment came in the 1966 FA Cup final when he took the winning goal very well; very calm and collected.

Jimmy Harris was no relation to Brian although he was another one from the Wirral. He was a good player, Jimmy. He was very fast and could play on the right wing or at centre forward. He took over from me when I went to Aston Villa and again for a few weeks when I went to Liverpool.

George Kirby was a young striker who came in after me, along with Jimmy Harris. Like all of the young players, you'd try and help them along the way. That's the way we did things at Everton, everyone helps everybody else. Eddie Thomas was not a bad inside forward, who went to Blackburn Rovers from Everton. He was a steady player. All the steady players would come in, you know, and they'd mix and match: Eddie Thomas, Gwyn Lewis, Eddie O'Hara. Not bad players at all, but not great either; not good enough to make a first-team shirt their own.

We started the 1958/59 season badly, losing the first six games. This run included a 6–1 hammering at home to Arsenal. 'This was a massacre at Goodison,' wrote Michael Charters in the Football *Echo*. 'Everton were completely outplayed at every point by a brilliant Arsenal team who gave them a footballing lesson, plus goals.' Only Derek Temple's consolation five minutes from the end prevented the record 0–6 Goodison defeats of 1912 and 1922 being equalled.

Soon after the board intervened and sacked Ian Buchan. While they deliberated on his replacement a three man sub-committee picked the team. It didn't really get much better without him – although I did score my best ever goal during this period!

We were playing West Bromwich Albion at the Hawthorns and my second of the afternoon was the winner in a 3–2 win. I ran from the halfway line with their centre half, Ray Barlow, chasing me. There were three or four players bearing down on me and I passed them all and scored. The *Daily Post's* Michael Charters gave a rather more colourful description in the following Monday's paper:

Dave with Bobby Collins and two young fans. He credited Collins with being the finest player he played alongside.

Bob Latchford
FORMER EVERTON NUMBER 9

Bob Latchford signed for Everton from Birmingham City in a British record transfer deal in 1974 that took Howard Kendall and Archie Styles to St Andrews. Over seven-and-a-half years at Goodison he scored 138 goals for Everton and is considered one of the club's greatest centre forwards. Here he recounts the responsibilities of being an Everton number nine – a tradition set by Dean, Lawton and, of course, Hickson.

When I first signed for Everton in 1974 I wasn't immediately aware of the club's great tradition of number nines. Very soon afterwards it became apparent, from being around the club and the players and staff, just how important the number nine jersey was to Evertonians. It was a challenge, to be honest, to be regarded as one of the better centre forwards.

Every centre forward is judged against the one true legend and icon of this club, William Ralph 'Dixie' Dean. I was fortunate to meet him a few times and he was a lovely, lovely man. Very softly spoken and not very tall – I was amazed how short he was! – but obviously he was my age now back then, in his sixties. He was the gold standard that all Everton centre forwards are judged against.

It is not just about scoring goals when you are an Everton number nine. It is about playing with bravery and passion and energy and showing the desire and commitment and the willingness to put yourself in situations where you are going to take bumps and scrapes. But on top of that, you've got to score, and that's ultimately what you are going to be judged on.

I didn't come into contact with Dave Hickson too much when I was playing. My knowledge came only really through what other players have said when he was around, that he was really a very hard, tough man, that he took no prisoners. It was very hard to imagine that he did some of the things he did on the football field if you ever met him. If you saw him you couldn't think it was possible, but apparently he was a tough cookie.

I can say that he was a wonderful man and I got to know him really well over the last ten years of his life. I knew him better as an 'ordinary human being' than as a footballer and he was a very passionate man. I think the club and fans instil that sort of passion into you. I have been around a few clubs but Evertonians are truly very, very special. They want to know about you, they want to know about their ex-players and what they are doing, and they are always so excited to see you. It amazes me every time I come back to see the passion they have still for their ex-players. I think that Dave appreciated that a lot.

I feel very proud to have played for Everton and to have been their number nine. I know how important it is. It is a great thing to be part of an unbroken tradition and to be part of a list that fans reel off: Dean, Lawton, Young, Pickering, Latchford, Sharp, Ferguson, and, of course, Dave Hickson.

Dave Cockram

FRIEND OF DAVE'S

Dave Cockram was a good friend of Dave Hickson's during the last decade of his life. A well-known member of the Ellesmere Port branch of the Everton Supporters Club, 'Cocky' often attended Goodison with Hickson and visited him at his home.

Being an Evertonian I was obviously aware of who Dave Hickson was and what he meant to everybody. My dad idolised him. His dad idolised him. Everyone did. He was a proper Everton icon. If someone doesn't know Dave Hickson, they don't know Everton. Dave was always known as 'Ellesmere Port's favourite son'. Like Joe Mercer, everyone from the town was proud he'd come from there.

Dave stood out for Evertonians because of his famous saying: 'I'd break every bone in my body for any club I played for, but I'd die for Everton.' Dave didn't say that for a one-line attention-seeking quote, he meant it; he played with his heart on his sleeve and would do anything for Everton.

He didn't have a bad bone in his body, but on the pitch he was as tough as anything. I was unfortunate not to be old enough to have seen Dave play, but my dad says he'd go through a brick wall for Everton. Joe Royle jokes that Dave would come off the pitch covered in blood, 'and sometimes it was even his own', which I think is a great saying.

He was a lovely man, but he had a stubborn streak too. It was never nasty, but he could dig his heels in. It was normally over Everton, to be honest! When he was unwell he'd be desperate to not just go to the match, but to work the lounges too. Even when we told him, 'Dave – people will come to you,' he wouldn't listen.

Dave was a one-off, but I think in Duncan Ferguson we came close to the sort of player he was. I know Dave loved watching Duncan and saw something of himself in him. Dave might not have been the greatest Everton player or have won anything, but I think he was probably the most loved player in the club's history. When I went to games with him, we'd spend more time outside the stadium signing autographs than we did inside. He wouldn't leave until all autographs had been signed and photographs had all been taken. I've seen young Evertonians, aged ten or eleven, walk past current players to get his autograph. It shows how stories about Dave have been passed down the generations. I think that tells you everything about the way in which he was considered.

I miss not being able to go to the match with Dave any more. But most of all I miss him as a friend.

Dave Hickson, Everton's great-hearted centre-forward, will never score a finer goal, or one more valuable to his club, than his wonder effort two minutes from the end of the game at the Hawthorns.

Every Albion player, except goalkeeper Jackman, was in Everton's half. They had just forced two successive corners. Thomas finally hooked the ball away from a penalty area scramble and it landed at Hickson's feet, on the edge of the centre circle in his own half.

The commanding, towering, masterful Ray Barlow stood alone between Hickson and Jackman in that far-off Albion goal; fully 50 yards away. The Albion backs were spread on either wing: the home half of the pitch was almost virgin territory if Hickson could beat Barlow. Could he do it?

Yes, he could and did. With a neat body-swerve to the right, he slipped around Barlow on the left, looked up and the Albion goal must have seemed to Hickson as though he was peering through the wrong end of a telescope.

Dragging down deep on his stamina, Hickson fled after the ball like a sprinter leaning forward to find every ounce of pace in his body. He reached the ball, pushed it another 20 yards ahead with Barlow, Setters and Dudley pounding after him, losing a little ground at every step.

Had he sent the ball too far with his last kick? Would Jackman, coming out from goal, reach the ball first? No. The goalkeeper was a little slow to sense the danger and Hickson came to the ball just outside the penalty area with Jackman some five yards away, narrowing the angle.

Hickson met the ball and shot in one flowing movement of his right foot. The ball sped low past Jackman's right hand and bulged the back of the net with every Everton player leaping and cavorting in joy, rushing to overwhelm Hickson with their congratulations.

I was absolutely shattered at the end of it. I should have kept on running because the other players all piled on top of me and almost crushed me to death in a mad celebration. People always remember my goals in the 1953 FA Cup run, but that was the best.

On 11 October 1958 we went to White Hart Lane, which was always one of my favourite stadiums. We came in on the back of three straight wins. What unfolded was one of the most extraordinary afternoons in English football history as 14 goals were shared between us. Unfortunately 10 of those went Tottenham's way, although we should have had 10 ourselves. Jimmy Harris scored a hat-trick but I should have had five. John Hollowbread, the Tottenham keeper, was in unbelievable form, and so too was Bobby Smith, the Spurs forward. It should have been 15–10 to Spurs because Bobby was unbelievable that day. It was a frustrating game because with new signing Bobby Collins in the side we were developing into the sort of team that could score lots of goals. We just couldn't keep them out.

Johnny Carey came in as manager from Blackburn Rovers. I had, of course, come up against him when he was a player with Manchester United. He was a nice fella, probably too nice to be a manager in some ways.

The key man, for me, was Bobby Collins. We had signed him from Celtic in the period between Buchan's dismissal and Carey's appointment. He was an inside forward and probably the best player I ever played alongside. We had a year or so together before I joined Liverpool and he was great. Bobby would play the early ball: he would get it and know exactly what you were doing, and play it where you wanted it. He was so clever. You couldn't ask for anything else from an inside forward. It was nice when you could get an understanding going with the rest of your forward line.

Bobby was also a winner. All of our players, in their way, were winners, but Bobby was the real deal. He was like me. He'd dive through crowds of players to get where he wanted and was ridiculously brave. He was hard. Although, like me, he was gone by the time Everton started lifting trophies under Harry Catterick, he helped bring a winning ethos back to Everton and also brought it to Leeds United, where he encountered lots of success.

Good partnerships are generally something that just happens. I think you've got to try and work on it as well, but you do just seem to know with some players. Liverpool have always seemed to have done well when putting those forward partnerships together: you had Hunt and St John, Toshack and Keegan, and now you've got Sturridge and Suarez. You can just see that they're meant to play together.

Derek Mountfield
FORMER EVERTON PLAYER

Derek Mountfield won two league titles, the FA Cup and European Cup Winners' Cup at the heart of Everton's defence in the mid-1980s, also playing for Tranmere Rovers, Aston Villa, Wolves, Carlisle United, Northampton, Walsall and Scarborough. After his retirement from football he became a close friend of Dave and Pat Hickson.

I believe yourself and your wife were very good friends with Dave Hickson, and used to take him to matches and dinners?
Derek Mountfield: I became very good friends with Dave, must be seven, eight or nine years ago. We used to travel in from Chester and go on to the games, and then I moved into Willaston. I lost my dad many years ago; Dave was like another dad to me, or a granddad. We got on great; we had a good relationship together. When Pat died it was difficult for Dave, it was like having his right arm chopped off basically, and I was there to do what I could, when I could. But it was an honour to do it – I really enjoyed it.

You say it was an honour, what was he like as a man?
DM: Where do I start? Obnoxious, cantankerous, a pain in the backside at times! He was a strange character. He had his own little ways. He was blue to the core, he had nothing bad said against Everton, nothing bad said about Pat. But when you got to know him he was a funny old bugger.

For someone that played for Everton a couple of generations after him, what was it like to be so close to someone who was a past great?
DM: For me it was that he was a very good friend of mine. It was quite strange, we just had no airs and graces about each other. I didn't see Dave as anything other than a mate. He wasn't Dave Hickson the Everton player from the 1950s and 1960s who played for both sides. He was just Dave.

It was always amazing how many people actually recognised Dave. I've taken him to both Aston Villa and Huddersfield Town and I was amazed how many people recognised him and swooped over like when he was outside Goodison Park.

When you were a player were you aware of him then? Did you know him personally?
DM: No, I didn't know him at all. It wasn't until the Former Players' Foundation came on board and I started to meet the players that I used to watch from the terraces. My dad used to talk about people like Alex Young and Brian Labone [but] as a former player you don't meet those people unless you go to functions. Until the Foundation came along I didn't really know any of the former players from whatever era, but now it's quite strange, it's put me in touch with a lot of people that I used to watch on the terraces and people that my dad used to talk about from the 1940s, 1950s and 1960s.

You played for Tranmere and Aston Villa like Dave, is he well thought of there?
DM: I do a lot of work with the former players there and I go down to a lot of games and they'd ask me to invite Dave down. So I took him down and was amazed at the number of people that recognised him. He played there in the late 50s and I was amazed how many people actually recognised him.

My wife and I took him and Pat over to Huddersfield every year to watch a game. One year they invited all four of us to the Tranmere game, Dave and Pat stayed in a hotel and I picked them up and got to the car park and it took us about an hour to get the best part of 400 yards because Dave was just mobbed by people.

It became a standing joke between Dave and Pat, me and my wife Julie; Dave always signed 'best wishes Dave Hickson' and then Pat would say, 'Hurry up, Dave, I need me dinner!' And so in the end we said to Dave, "Forget the best wishes and just sign "Dave Hickson".' It became a standing joke over the years whenever he said, 'Should I just sign best wishes?' We'd reply, 'No, you're fine!'

It was always the same, before we could get anywhere near the ground, the respect and the aura around him. He was just an amazing person.
Interview by George Gibson

Football by the late 1950s was starting to change. You could sense it. There was a bit of money coming into the game, and things were being run a bit more professionally. John Moores, the Littlewoods tycoon, had started to put a bit of money into Everton. Goodison was a fine old ground, but it started to get better, with floodlights and so on. His investment had an impact on the pitch as well, with new signings. There was a sense of change, but you could never have envisaged it would be the way it is now. There was a board, a manager and they were in complete control of the club, the team, and your destiny; it was strict and you had to abide by it.

One of the developments in football at this time was floodlights. Night games were the most dramatic. Everton introduced floodlights in 1957, four tall lights on stanchions in each corner of the ground. I played in the first floodlit games at Goodison and Anfield in 1957 in rare Mersey derby encounters in this period. After they built them and we'd play at night something would happen to the crowd. They were electrified. It was magical. I looked forward to them greatly, I'd be lying awake the night before looking forward to it. I couldn't wait for it to start. Once you were on the pitch you were all right. It was that build-up. The crowd were fantastic.

You go to Goodison now for a night game when it's full and there'll be 38 or 39,000 there. Imagine doubling that? It was unbelievable. I'll always remember playing Charlton Athletic in the fourth round of the FA Cup in 1959. We drew 2–2 at their place and brought them back to Goodison the following Wednesday; 74,782 filled Goodison that night and the lights were on, not that all those people could have seen much. Thick, dense fog filled the pitch. We won 4–1 after extra time, having drawn 1–1 at 90 minutes; I scored a couple but there was just confusion. People were shouting out, 'Davey, who scored that one?' Even I wasn't sure!

Everton made it through to a fifth round home tie against Aston Villa on 14 February. I scored again, but it was a Valentine's Day massacre as we lost 4–1 to a Villa team that would be relegated that season. It was a bit like that at Everton under Johnny Carey. Relegation for Everton was easily averted in 1959 and we finished sixteenth – the same we had the previous season.

Carey, for all his niceness, dropped me early in the 1959/60 season. We hadn't won any of the first six games and the pressure was on. I scored both goals when we beat Sheffield Wednesday 2–1 in mid-September, and Johnny was talking me up for an England cap. But the corner still hadn't really been turned. The following month we lost consecutive games 1–0 to West Ham and Chelsea and I was out of the team.

Johnny made it clear that he wanted to sell me, and he called me into his office.

'Plymouth Argyle have come in for you,' he said. 'Would you like to go there?'

Plymouth was about as far away as you could get from Merseyside.

'Not really,' I said. 'No.'

Crowd congestion when Everton played Charlton Athletic in an FA Cup fourth round replay in January 1959. Nearly 75,000 fans crammed into Goodison to see a 4-1 victory, Dave scoring twice

Alec Farrall
FOOTBALLER AND FRIEND

Alec Farrall entered the Everton first team as a 17-year-old midfielder at the end of the 1952/53 season. He made one appearance in each of the four subsequent campaigns, before joining Preston North End in 1957. After nearly lifting the League Championship at Deepdale in his first season he forged a successful lower-league career with Gillingham, Lincoln and Watford. Now in his seventies, he still attends Goodison to see his first club.

Dave was always very friendly with me. When I broke into the team I was 17, he'd be about 25. He seemed a grown-up man to me. But he was always friendly to me, Davey.

There were quite a few of us from the Wirral who played for Everton in the 1950s. Myself, Jimmy Harris – who still goes to the matches every Saturday and I see when Everton's at home – Brian Harris with whom I used to play in the Wirral Schoolboys, John Willie Parker, Kenny Birch and, of course, Davey. I'm not really sure why the Wirral was so well represented at the time. When you are kids you just play football; you don't know who's watching you.

Life as a footballer was entirely different than it is today, entirely different. You played because you enjoyed it, you never gave it too much thought, even when we played in front of huge crowds. I played my first game when Dave was centre forward; it was in the Second Division at home to Lincoln City and we got rightly hammered, 3–0.

I had a lot of injuries from the age of 17 to 21. I had three operations on my knee and I lost all confidence; and that's when the directors put me on the transfer list. I suppose I deserved it because I wasn't playing very well. I think they could have given me another year because of the trouble I had with my knee but they didn't really know anything about football.

After we finished playing from time to time I used to go for a meal with Dave and his wife, and Joe Mercer too. He was great with me; a really smashing lad.

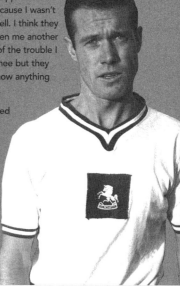

I didn't know how I was good enough for England just a few weeks earlier and now only good enough for Plymouth. But as a footballer you didn't really have any say in your destiny, so I went down anyway to have a look. I wasn't really interested in joining Plymouth at all. I was also adamant that I wasn't going to ask for a transfer this time.

The supporters weren't happy with my omission and filled both my postbag and that of the local press with letters of protest. 'The dropping of Hickson astounds me,' wrote R. Almond of Geneva Road, Liverpool 6, to the *Echo*. 'Why could not Shackleton have played inside-right? The players' patience must be stretched to breaking point at the way they are being pushed around. Swapping and changing has already lost two Everton players international caps and Hickson's omission knocks at least 5,000 off the attendance without adding to the team's effectiveness …'

Hickson returned to the Everton team for a visit to Leeds United on 10 October 1959. He demonstrated that he still, indisputably, had what it took to succeed in the top flight, scoring a brace in a 3–3 draw. 'Hickson scored two in a

style which no one else on Everton's books could achieve …' reported the Echo. 'He took a pass from Shackleton, swerved around full back Ashall and Charlton in a Collins-style dribble, and took the ball along the by-line. With goalkeeper Wood expecting a cross, Hickson took the chance to slam home a shot through the narrowest of gaps with unerring accuracy.'

These were the last goals the Cannonball Kid ever scored for Everton.

Billy Butler

BBC RADIO MERSEYSIDE DJ

One of the best-known and most well-loved personalities in Liverpool, Billy Butler's career as a DJ extends for more than half a century from when he worked in the Cavern Club. The voice of BBC Radio Merseyside, Billy is a lifelong Evertonian who grew up in the 1950s idolising Dave Hickson. In later life he played alongside Dave in charity games and became a good friend.

The 1950s were a difficult era: you had war damage, austerity, rationing. What did Dave Hickson mean to people like you growing up in Liverpool?
Billy Butler: What it meant was having a hero, especially for me, I suppose, because I didn't have a dad. So Dave Hickson was my hero.

Dave Hickson wasn't just a footballer, he was a story-book footballer. He was the kind of footballer you read about but doesn't really exist – but he did! Every Saturday afternoon we used to go and watch him play, even at Liverpool – because I had such high regard for him as a player.

Unlike today's pass-pass-pass football, when Dave Hickson got the ball, he regarded it as his duty to score and he just headed straight to the goal. Even later on in life, when Dave played for my charity team in the Isle of Man in the 1980s, when we went out on the drinks until midnight, Dave got up at ten o'clock and says, 'I'm going to bed, we gotta game tomorrow.' That's how seriously he took it. I'll always remember playing against the Isle of Man Police and Dave was brilliant. When he came off, I said, 'Great game, Dave.' He replied, 'Nah, nah, I didn't score. As a centre forward it's my job to score.' That's just the way he saw football.

He played for the Billy Butler Charity XI on a few occasions, and I'll always remember the first time. He passed the ball to me, and I totally missed it because I was so completely overawed because Dave Hickson had passed the ball to me!

Was he still a hard player when he was playing as a veteran?
BB: Oh yeah! He still took no prisoners when he played. He complained a lot as well and he even did that in his younger days.

When he was playing for Everton, you said he was a story-book footballer. What was it about him? Was it the quiff?
BB: It was the hair, it was the looks. It was the fact that he

seemed to be able to float on air when he went up for headers. He was just the centre forward you read about as far as I was concerned. You knew he was playing for Everton; you knew his heart was in the game. There wouldn't be a minute in the ninety that he wasn't trying to win for Everton.

Where would you watch Everton games from?
BB: It would have been the boys' pen initially, then we'd climb over. In those days it was a little bit difficult climbing over; you'd have to get someone holding you up onto the stanchions to help you up.

Would you know what was going on, would you know that Dave's head would be splattered with blood, or would you read about it the next day?
BB: Not really. Well, you knew something was up because he had a bandage on, but at the very, very back of the Gwladys Street you can't make out things brilliantly.

Football does take unexpected twists. Shortly after, Phil Taylor the Liverpool manager called me up and said, 'We'd like to sign you.' It was like the time I joined Villa. I was out of the side and just wanted to play. 'We'll play you every week,' he promised, and he did. That's how the move to Liverpool materialised. As far as I was concerned it was quite straightforward.

Because I was a professional I accepted it to a certain extent, but of course I was bitterly disappointed by this because I knew I'd have to move on again. I didn't want to leave. I came back to Goodison because I wanted to finish my career there. I think what did for me again was my disciplinary record. Everton didn't like players who were booked or sent off. That wasn't the image the directors wanted to present. My record, in fairness, wasn't that bad, given that football was a very physical game at the time and I was a physical player.

People sometimes ask me if I'd adapt to football today. They seem to think that because I was so physical I'd be sent off all the time. But I'd have been fine. You adapt in life, in all sorts of situations. I would have been a slightly different player, I suppose, but I'd have done just fine in today's Premier League, if I felt as though I was being protected from defenders. But if the

October 31, 1988

Birthday blasts from the past for soccer ace Dave

by Chris James

DAVE Hickson, that old soccer warhorse from the fifties, got a birthday surprise on Saturday as he celebrated his 60th birthday at the Southend Social Club in Rock Ferry.

To Dave's surprise, he was suddenly surrounded by many of his old soccer friends from the past including Harry Leyland, Jimmy Tansey, Tommy Jones, Ken Birch, Jimmy Harris and Tony McNamara.

It was all part of a special treat for Hickson who

starred for Everton, Aston Villa, Liverpool and Huddersfield in the fifties and still plays regularly in charity matches.

Hickson, who still works for his town council in Ellesmere Port trains twice a week to keep himself in condition and still sports the blond hair which made him an unmistakeable player while he was a player.

During an emotional evening, Hickson was also played a tape with congratulatory messages from many other big names and former team mates of the fifties.

Taken aback – Dave contemplates his surprise evening with wife Pat and organiser Ossie Armour

defenders are going a bit gung ho, you'd want to give them a little bit back to let them to know you were playing the game too. That's all it was about. No malice, no nothing. I didn't want to hurt anybody, or take anybody's legs. I just wanted to play hard football.

I made plain my frustrations with Everon in an interview shortly before completing the switch to Anfield.

I've been forced into it and you will understand that no one can play his best in these circumstances.

The club have signed two centre-forwards in the past 18 months – first Peter Harburn and then Alan Shackleton – and although I was prepared at the outset to fight my way back into the team, I now feel that the feeling against me is too strong.

They've knocked the life out of me and I'm prepared to go. I'm not in love with playing for Everton any more.

Don't forget that this is not the first time being played in the Reserve side at Newcastle has led to my asking for a move.

It happened in 1955 when Cliff Britton was the guvnor here.

That dropping led to my being transferred to Aston Villa and later to Huddersfield Town. So the wheel has turned full circle.

I've been at Goodison Park since I was 14 and Everton have always been my club but I cannot help thinking that the feeling against me in certain quarters when I rejoined Everton from Huddersfield Town two

DAVE HICKSON

seasons ago is still acting against me.

I feel I am being made a scapegoat and a stop gap and I'm not prepared to be either.

My chat this morning with Mr Carey was quite amicable, but I feel a change would help to renew my form and my interest in the game.

It is obvious that they are trying to throw me out. Why didn't they let me go to Liverpool three weeks ago when I was dropped so that Shackleton could be brought in? Why did they stand in my way?

I know Liverpool were interested and I would have gone to them. As things have turned out I shall lose the £300 due to any player whose club transfers him 'without consent'.

I love football and I love fans, and I feel there is a danger, in view of what has happened, that fans will begin to believe that they are getting rid of me because I am a troublemaker.

That is not so. You know that there has never been any complaint or reason for complaint of this kind.

Was he any good?
BB: I always thought so, yes. Dave was very unfortunate that in his day there were hardly any videos and stuff like that, so there's hardly anything to judge him by. The main things you have are photos, and when you see the photos of him in midair and going up for goals, and you see his determination – they often say as much as a moving picture could.

How did you feel when he left?
BB: I felt dreadful. I couldn't understand what Everton were doing. As far as I was concerned, he was the man, the heart and soul of Everton. But when he went to Liverpool, I was quite pleased about that because it meant I could still watch him!

I'd never have done that before Dave because I couldn't really afford it, but with Dave, we made an exception. You'd do a few more messages, take your papers back to the chippy, take some empty bottles back so you got a bit of extra money. To me it is still one of the best sights in football; him and Roger Hunt going forward, because Hunty was very much the same as him with the hair and everything. They looked great going together.

After he left, did anybody ever replace him in your heart?
BB: I was probably a bit too old for that then. I wasn't at the right age to want another hero.

What was it like later on in life, getting to know him?
BB: I got to know him because I used to play alongside him, but apparently he used to listen to my programme and really liked it. The embarrassing thing was that when I first met Dave he was treating me as if I was something special. I found that hard to cope with. If I ever played a birthday dedication for him, he would be effusive with his thanks. I used to be embarrassed sometimes by the affection he used to show for me!

What's your principal memory of him playing for Everton? Is there one moment perhaps not recorded in the history books that you particularly recall?
BB: The first time I ever cried over a footy match was when I was about eleven and we got beat by Bolton in the FA Cup semi-finals. We didn't have radio at the time and I was listening to the neighbours' up the road. When they belatedly turned it on it was 4–0 – because they only used to broadcast the second half in those days. We got back to 4–3, and missed a penalty, but couldn't get a fourth goal. I cried my fecking eyes out because of the tension. We were in the Second Division and had done so well to get so close.

Later, I remember him stepping out of the fog against Charlton in an FA Cup tie. It was hard to see anything at all, but he came out of the fog and scored.

Later on in life he was great company. He had a great football mind, his memory for football facts and figures was brilliant. As you know, he was 245 million per cent Everton through and through. It was funny to go out with him: he always had a little cigar in his pocket to offer you. Then there was the famous Dave Hickson £5 notes. He always had a fiver in his top pockets ready to buy a drink, but I don't think it was ever used because in company – such was the reverence in which he was held – he hardly ever had to buy anybody a drink.

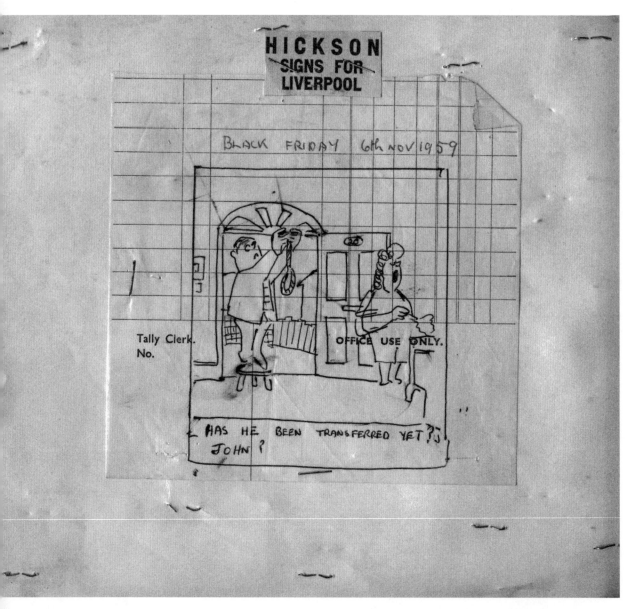

This cartoon, drawn by Crosby-based fan, John Norman, and found in Hickson's belongings when he died typified the mood at the time of Dave's departure in 1959.

I was aware of all the controversy surrounding my departure, that there were Evertonians vowing never to go back to Goodison and Liverpool fans promising never to go to Anfield. One letter signed by 60 fans made plain people's anger at the move:

> **We who come here every week to see the strongest side Everton can field are becoming tired of being given second best because of prejudices in certain quarters. Even if players are not available from outside to strengthen the team, at least let us have the best one on the books. You [Everton] appear to be the only people of the opinion that Shackleton is better than Hickson.**

An Agreement made the Sixth

day of November 19⁵⁹ between J.S. Mc Innes of Anfield Read, Liverpool 4

in the COUNTY OF Lancaster

the Secretary of and acting pursuant to Resolution and Authority for and on

behalf of the LIVERPOOL FOOTBALL CLUB

of LIVERPOOL (hereinafter referred to as the Club)

of the one part and DAVID HICKSON

of 78 Mostyn Avenue, Aintree, Liverpool 10.

in the COUNTY OF LANCASTER Professional Football Player

(hereinafter referred to as the Player) of the other part **Whereby** it is agreed

as follows:—

1. The Player hereby agrees to play in an efficient manner and to the best of his ability for the Club.

2. The Player shall attend the Club's ground or any other place decided upon by the Club for the purposes of or in connection with his training as a Player pursuant to the instructions of the Secretary, Manager, or Trainer of the Club, or of such other person, or persons, as the Club may appoint. (This provision shall not apply if the Player is engaged by the Club at a weekly wage of less than One Pound, or at a wage per match.)

3. The Player shall do everything necessary to get and keep himself in the best possible condition so as to render the most efficient service to the Club, and will carry out all the training and other instructions of the Club through its representative officials.

4. The Player shall observe and be subject to all the Rules, Regulations and Bye-Laws of The Football Association, and any other Association, League, or Combination of which the Club shall be a member. And this Agreement shall be subject to any action which shall be taken by The Football Association under their Rules for the suspension or termination of the Football Season, and if any such suspension or termination shall be decided upon the payment of wages shall likewise be suspended or terminated, as the case may be.

5. The Player shall not engage in any business or live in any place which the Directors (or Committee) of the Club may deem unsuitable.

6. If the Player shall be guilty of serious misconduct or breach of the disciplinary Rules of the Club, the Club may, on giving 14 days' notice to the said Player, or the Club may, on giving 28 days' notice to the said Player,

"It's coming to a **Liverpudlian** Anfield for so-

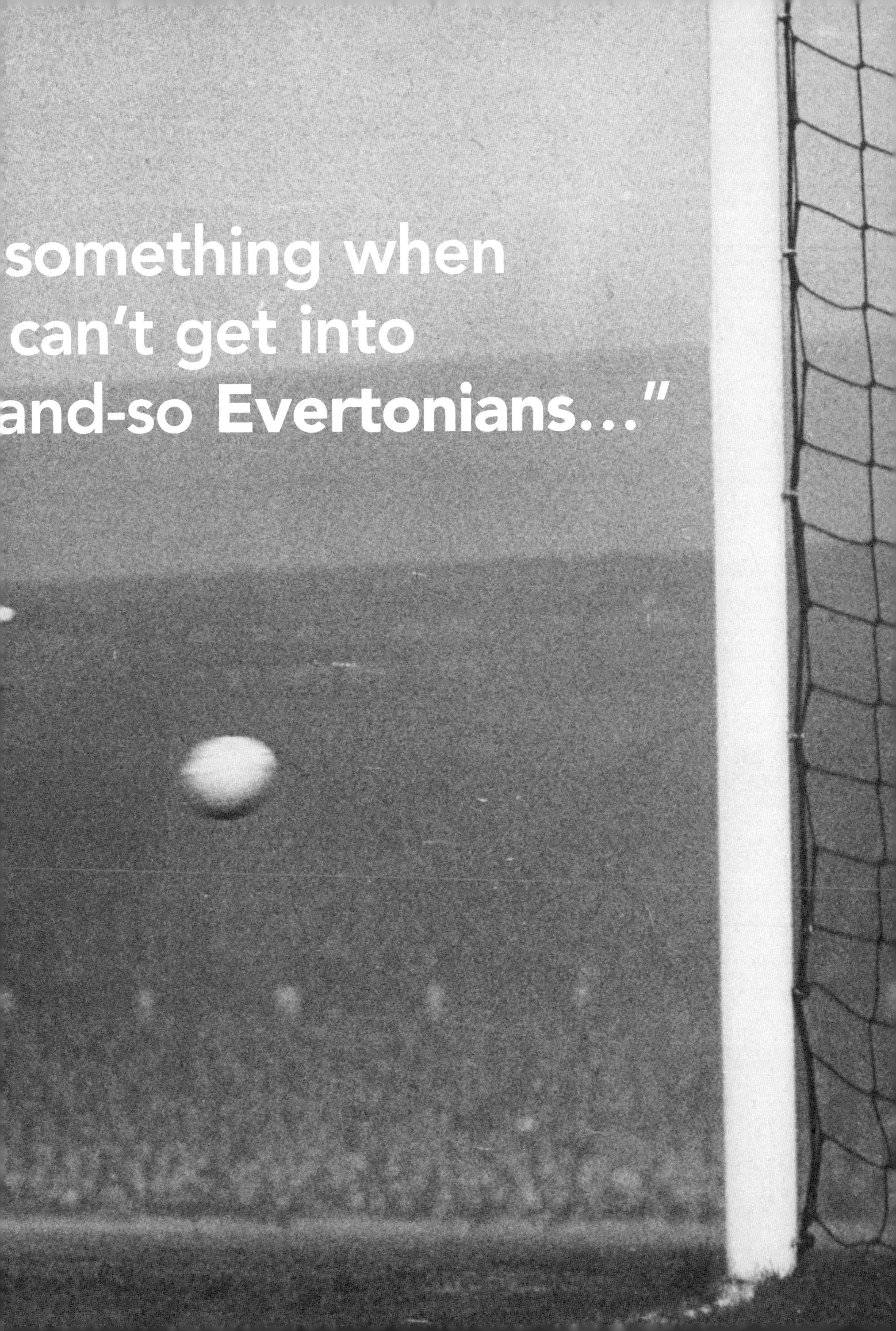

something when
can't get into
and-so Evertonians..."

Roger Hunt
LIVERPOOL FORWARD

Roger Hunt was most famous for being in the England side that won the 1966 World Cup, but he also had a distinguished career at Liverpool. Hunt is the club's all-time record league goalscorer with 245 goals in 404 league games. When Dave Hickson moved to Liverpool in 1959, he partnered Hunt in attack.

What are your memories of playing against Everton?
Roger Hunt: I enjoyed playing against Everton. There was always a rivalry with Liverpool but the local derbies, they were always – they still are, aren't they? – big occasions.

So how did the Liverpool players take it when Dave Hickson signed for the club?
RH: Liverpool were in the Second Division and the players welcomed Dave because obviously he was a noted goalscorer. I hadn't been in the team all that long and he was great, we played well together. He scored quite a lot of goals when he came to Liverpool.

What was it like to play alongside him?
RH: He was very good in the air. I used to play alongside him, maybe just behind. He was tough, he was hard and he was always desperate to score goals. And if he didn't score a goal, even if the team won, he wasn't all that happy. He was desperate to score. I partnered him and I think we got 20-odd goals apiece, something like that. He was great to play with.

Did you see much of him after he left Liverpool?
RH: Well, I tried to keep in touch with him from time to time and I went to his funeral because I did appreciate what he did at Liverpool even though he didn't stay for very long. It was before Bill Shankly arrived when Dave came to Liverpool and they had worked together when he was assistant manager at Huddersfield and I don't know if they got on very well.

Did you enjoy playing alongside him?
RH: Very much, yeah, because he was a goalscorer and I was. We understood each other on the field, where to go, and we both scored quite a few goals in that period.

How would he rank alongside other centre forwards that you played with? The likes of Geoff Hurst...
RH: He was a really top-class centre forward, an all-round goalscorer. He was right up there with the best goalscorers.

'This was essentially a now-or-never signing, aimed at allowing Liverpool to strike out for a challenging position in their Division, and at promotion,' wrote Leslie Edwards. 'Never in the history of football in this city has there been such a rumpus about a player from one club joining neighbours and rivals. Everton fans have written that if Hickson goes they go with him; Liverpool have received warning that if Hickson arrives some of their most loyal fans will depart!'

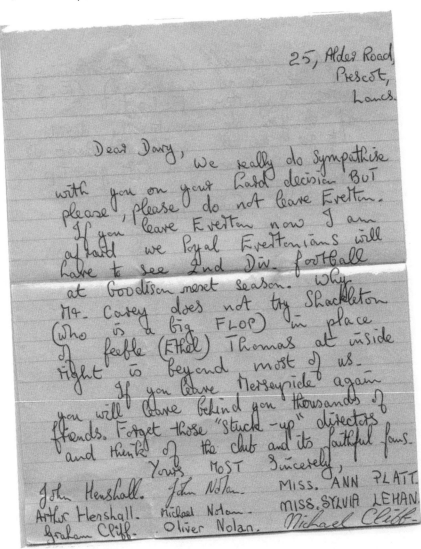

I received many many letters from Evertonians imploring me to stay. 'We really do sympathise with you on your hard decision BUT please, please do not leave Everton. If you leave Everton now I am afraid we loyal Evertonians will have to see 2nd Div football at Goodison next season,' recorded one letter that was signed by no fewer than nine fans from Prescot. 'I am so utterly disgusted at the treatment meted out to you by your club, that I felt I must write to you with much affection and all my sympathy, and to your club to express my feelings toward them, and to withdraw my support after all this long time,' wrote a Mr Chadwick of Childwall, a supporter of 30 years standing. 'I can go back to the Dixie Dean and Tommy Lawton eras, but you can take it from me that neither of these great men was held with more affection than yourself by the great majority of Evertonians.' 'Please stay with Everton,' wrote yet another

7 Lathom Ave.
Wallasey.

Dear Dave,
I can't tell you how disgusted I am with the happenings of this last week. I have been an Everton supporter since 1945, we have not had much to cheer about in this time in fact your play is one of the few things that we have had to cheer about.

It seems that a certain faction on the Board have got their way, but I assure you Dave the fans are not with them, I see you are quoted as saying you have lost your love for playing for Everton, I am not surprised after past events, but despite all this Dave, always remember the true supporters never wavered in their admiration for your enthusiastic and whole hearted play.

The Best of luck Dave in which ever colours you are going to wear, even if it be the red of Liverpool (a situation I never dreamt would arise). but to me you will always be an Evertonian.

Yours Sincerely,
Norman Costain

Dave received hundreds of letters from both Evertonians and Liverpudlians at the time of his 1959 transfer.

PERSONAL. To Dave Hickson.
Mr Arthur Wescombe.
27 Nebo Street
Wavertree
Liverpool, 15.
Saturday. Nov 7th 1959.

Dear Dave,
As a Liverpool supporter for 30 years, since I was 10 year of age, as one of the 50,000 who was at the match this afternoon, I would like to say "Welcome to Anfield" and, may you stay with us for the rest of your football career. Thank you to yourself and your wife for sticking out to

②
stay in Liverpool, I admire your "guts" and loyalty and may I wish all the Luck in the world and God Bless you and your wife who must be very proud of in helping you out in your trying time. I wish you had come to Liverpool 2 years ago. After to-days display I feel very confident for the League and Cup. all the Best. Dave
Yours Sincerely
A. Wescombe
P.S. 2 golden goals today. Take no notice of the "knockers"

group of young supporters. 'It would not be right for you to play for Liverpool

The majority of Liverpool supporters were very kind. 'Welcome to Anfield,' wrote Arthur Wescombe of Wavertree, ' and may you stay with us for the rest of your football career.' I did, however, have a few phone calls from Liverpool fans, nothing too nasty, but warning me, 'You'll never replace our Billy.' Our Billy was, of course, Billy Liddell. Some Evertonians came over to Anfield just to see me play, including a young Bill Kenwright. One lady wrote to me after my Liverpool debut saying: 'My husband and I were really delighted on Sat when Liverpool won and even more pleased when you scored both goals. We are both Everton supporters or at least I was when you were there.' That sort of thing made me feel proud, very proud indeed.

At the time it had to go over my head really, but I was concerned about it. I often look back, even now, and think, why did this happen? How did I end up at Anfield? People knew I grew up with Everton and suddenly I was there on the other side of the park. It was strange really, but it's not something I've regretted. I enjoyed playing for Liverpool because I enjoyed playing football. However, put me against the wall and ask, 'Who would you like to play for?' and I've always got to say, 'Everton.' I was 14 when I started at Everton and it's like going to your first school. You go there and always remember it.

Kevin Lewis
FORMER LIVERPOOL FORWARD

When winger Kevin Lewis joined Liverpool in June 1960 it united him with a fellow son of Ellesmere Port in Hickson. The pair combined well for a season in a free-scoring forward line, although in May 1961 a report in the Liverpool Echo erroneously claimed that the pair were to quit football and go into business together. Dave did in fact leave Liverpool the following month, but Lewis remained at Anfield for two more years, before playing for Huddersfield and Port Elizabeth City in South Africa, where he still lives.

There was a story at the end of Dave's time at Liverpool that I've never been able to get to the bottom of. It suggested that Dave and I were to leave the club and go into business together. I knew that Dave was moving to Cambridge; he was given a free transfer so he could go to Cambridge. He liked the idea; it was a nice place to go to. He was at the end of his career and it was a good move. That's all I'm aware of. I still to this day don't know how my name was mentioned in the story. It was a load of rubbish.

Dave was a character, I can say this. He was great to play alongside. He was a very good player. Skillful player; strong player. He was always talking, winding up opposing players, winding up his own teammates. Sometimes it was frustrating and sometimes it was helpful. He didn't always get on with Bill Shankly, who had inherited him when Huddersfield manager and inherited him again at Anfield.

The first time I played away from home, for some reason I shared a room with Dave Hickson, I think probably because we both came from the same town. But that was an education in itself. I can always remember him lying on the bed and he's singing nursery rhymes! I was saying, 'I can't get to sleep here, Dave, shut up, let's get some sleep.' But he goes on singing his nursery rhymes. Then suddenly in the middle of the night he heard the noise of a plane outside. He ran to the window and shouted, 'It's all right, Kev, it's one of ours!' How I played the next day I don't know, because I had no sleep that night whatsoever.

He used to keep himself to himself off the pitch, but because we both came from Ellesmere Port I knew him quite well. I remember going around to his house and was watching the horse racing on TV. Dave would have this idea which horse was going to win a race, so he would say, 'I'm backing number four or number five.' We'd be watching the TV and the commentator would say, 'This horse is looking very well.' Dave, straight away, would get on to the telephone and bet on that horse. Then somebody else on the TV would make a comment about a different horse and he'd be back on the phone to bet on that horse! He finished up backing about five horses in the same race! And you daren't – and I mean daren't –cheer for another horse that he hadn't backed otherwise he'd kick you out of the house.

But in that way he was fabulous, a character. If he was playing today they'd love him. He'd be on the front page – never mind the back – virtually every weekend. He was that type of character.

With his long hair, his skill, his volleying, the way he carried on when he was on the field was brilliant. The crowd would love him.

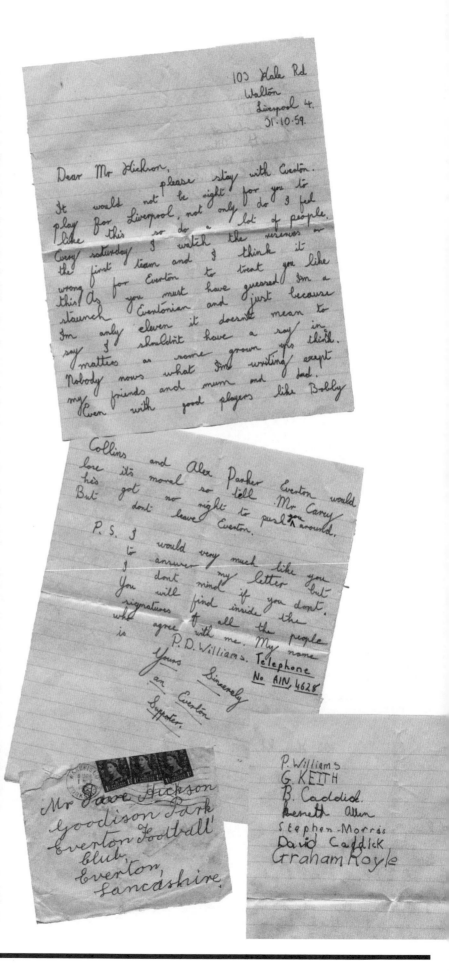

41, Grey Rock St
Liverpool 6.

Dear Dave, I hope you don't mind me writing at a time like this, But I am really anoyed with Everton's board, I really hope you leave Everton, I am not saying this because I don't like you, because I like you alot. But after getting dropt for the third time I wouldn't mind if a player took your place, but Shackelton as far as I am concerned (I think I have spelled that word wrong) as a player, he STINKS, as a friend off the field, I belive he's a nice lad, I hope he dosen't get anoyed with me. Well Dave I hope you go to Liverpool or any Lancashire clb, So I can go and watch you. But I really hope Collins and Parker go next, because they are too good for Everton, look at some of the tricks he does and some of the passes he gives Shackelton, Thomas and Harris J, look who is leading goalscorer, you are, and they drop you, no

2/
wonder Rainhill is full up. I hope this letter dosen't Start any trouble at the ground. There is nothink and thousands of more would like than, to see a forward line like this WAINWRIGHT, FIELDING, HICKSON PARKER AND EGLINGTON, only for that forward line mostly you and Parker, Everton would still be in the second Div. they should never of Farrell go or Lindsay. Well Dave the gates will go down alot, before long the Supporters will be getting prayed 2/ to go in. the Everton Selectors could help Merseyside a lot if they went to work on the docks where the strike is, It's a wonder they haven't drop Collins and put Harry Cooke in his place I hope Harry Cakes this. Well you keep this letter to your self if you can. I will be sorry I put all these nasty thenks after a while, but at this moment

3/
there is plenty of things I would like to say. Well Dave there is nothink more to say now, so don't forget don't go to far from Merseyside. So for now

cheerio

George Heywood.
P.S. Remember me to Tansy, and O'neill.

Despite the controversy there were huge queues waiting to get into Anfield for my debut against Aston Villa. With an attendance of nearly 50,000 Liverpool had 11,000 more fans than at any other league match so far that season. I scored two goals and I think that helped win a lot of Liverpool supporters over. I remember one fan running onto the pitch and saying, 'You're one of ours now.'

One journalist added: 'One rabid Liverpudlian, disgusted at having two Anfield doors closed in his face on Saturday, told me: "It's coming to something when a Liverpudlian can't get into Anfield for so-and-so Evertonians …"'

'It was the day on which fans at Anfield took him to their hearts as one of their own. And I never thought that possible,' wrote Edwards. 'This match will be recalled, years hence, as an occasion in the category of Dean's sixtieth-goal-in-a-season against Arsenal. "The day Dave came to Anfield," they will begin, nostalgically, long after the hero of the match has hung up his boots and ceased to be the most enigmatical figure in the game.'

I could tell straight away that Liverpool had some really talented young players, like Ian Callaghan and Roger Hunt, and that they just needed time. You could see right away that they were going to be really good players. I was very proud in my part helping these lads progress into being top players – even if Evertonians might not agree! Billy Liddell, who had been an idol of mine, was still turning out in the Liverpool forward line. Ronnie Moran, who would serve the club so well as a player and a coach, was there.

There was some exciting football being played at Anfield at the time, but it wasn't always winning football. Just a month after my arrival the Liverpool board sacked Phil Taylor as manager. Who should they replace him with, but my old boss at Huddersfield, Bill Shankly. People talk about Shankly today as if he was a god. As a man, he was all right. As a manager he was determined. He wanted results now. He was dedicated as well. To him, nobody was better than the team he had. Nobody was as good as Liverpool. It was great motivation.

He was good at building up team spirit too, which managers didn't really work at in those days. I remember we used to go to Blackpool for pre-season training and work as hard as dogs. But then he'd take us to see the greyhounds, just to get out of it all, and do something different to change the mood. It was fantastic.

Shankly was always all right with me, but each time I was under his management I was somebody else's signing. It was a strange position to be in. He had his own ideas and his own players and eventually his own signings. He sought change and I accepted that. That's the way it is and you can't fault that. He brought in Ian St John, who was to be my replacement.

We had a good team at Liverpool and although we didn't get promoted we played well. I knew from my time at Everton just how hard it was to get out of the Second Division. In each of my two years at Anfield we fell just short, finishing third – which a few years later would be good enough to secure promotion and nowadays would get you into the playoffs.

We should have gone up to the First Division. I'll always remember the game we slipped up, against Cardiff City when we got beaten 4–0 at home. It was unbelievable really. Then after I left they finally went up and made history under Bill Shankly.

Perhaps because he was so synonymous with Everton FC, and maybe because his relationship with Bill Shankly was never so close, Dave tended to underplay his achievements at Anfield. However, he was in some of the most prolific form of his career while a Liverpool player, scoring 21 league goals in just 27 appearances in his first season at the club and 16 in 33 games in his second season.

8th February 1960

Statement by David Hickson.

I am sorry that the Commission think I was guilty of the offence for which Mr Pickles sent me off the field as, in my own mind, I was not guilty.

In asking for leniency, I would say that my previous troubles have been that I was too free with my tongue. Since I came to Liverpool, I have made every endeavour to control my feelings in every way and have largely been successful, although some of the opposing players have tried my patience very sorely, knowing that they could hammer me without my being able to retaliate.

By nature I have been a somewhat dashing player, which has been of value to my Club, but now that I am advanced in my career, I really am trying to replace dash with skill and hope my Manager thinks I am successful in this.

If I am to be punished, I hope it will not be suspension as I really feel I am getting on top of my faults and not likely to offend again.

Within weeks of joining Liverpool, Dave had been sent off again, this time for a foul in front of the Kop. An unlikely alliance of Everton and Liverpool fans bombarded the FA, calling for leniency. This is Dave's appeal.

Dave never played with anything but the same verve and intensity that had characterised his career in the blue of Everton. Even when he was playing in Billy Liddell's testimonial he was reported seizing the ball 'like a hungry lion and smashing it into the net with something approaching venom'. Liverpudlians, it seemed, took this style of play to their hearts in the same way their neighbours once had. When Hickson was sent off during a 3–0 victory over Sheffield United in 1960, Hickson left Anfield in tears while a mob of several hundred fans had to be dispersed from the club car park while chanting, 'We want the referee.' Everton and Liverpool fans then united in petitioning the FA and seek the overturning of a violent conduct charge. The FA were sufficiently moved by this unprecedented show of unity to clear Hickson.

Shankly dropped Hickson in March 1961. It came at a time when he was linked with a reunion with Cliff Britton, by then manager of Preston North End. His absence from the team coincided with a dip in form that might ultimately have contributed to Liverpool's failure to get promotion at the end of the season. Never one to like being dropped, Dave requested a transfer, with Halifax Town and Crewe Alexandra said to be interested ahead of

the transfer deadline, but they were sufficiently deterred by the £10,000 asking price – a colossal fee for clubs of their standing.

Dave remained at Anfield and made a goalscoring return to the Liverpool team on 31 March 1961. However, Liverpool won just two of their last seven games of the 1960/61 season and missed out on promotion by six points.

After scoring in his last home game for Liverpool – a 3–0 win over Stoke – Dave was left out of the final game of the season and announced his intention to quit football. A statement was circulated saying that he and a

Dave's Liverpool payslip and a bank statement from the same period show just how basic player remuneration was in 1960.

Liverpool Football Club & Athletic Grounds Co. Ltd.

TELEPHONES:
ANFIELD 2361/2

MANAGER:
W. SHANKLY
SECRETARY:
J. S. McINNES

ANFIELD ROAD
LIVERPOOL 4

3rd May 1961.

D.Hickson. Esq.
1 Harrow Drive.
Liverpool 10.

Dear Dave   ,

     I am instructed by my Directors to inform you that
they regret they are unable to offer you a re-engagement for Season
1961/62 and have placed you on the Open-to-Transfer List, at a fee of
£ 7,000.(Seven Thousand Pounds)

     My Directors desire me to thank you for the loyal
services you have rendered during your association at Anfield, and they
hope you will soon be successful in securing an engagement with
another Club.

     I shall be happy to assist you in any way possible.

Yours sincerely,

J.S.McInnes

Secretary.

When he passed away, Dave left behind a huge collection of photographs and documents, some of which are included in this book. These include photographs of him (clockwise from top left) as a young boy; relaxing at home; socialising with friends; and playing for his battalion in Egypt.

Although the most Dave ever earned from football was only slightly more than his father took home from his job at Bowater's printing plant, it was enough to buy him a car. By the time he gained his first driving license in 1953 he was one of the most famous footballers in England.

Top: On his wedding day with Pat in 1986. Presenting Bill Kenwright with the letter he had once sent him as a schoolboy on This is Your Life.

Bottom: With the Rev. Harry Ross and Pat, who was a great friend to the couple.

Top: Success at Wembley at last in the 1995 veterans cup.

Below: An iconic picture of Dave in the Main Stand in the mid-noughties emerged in the days after his death. It became a social media hit, although its photographer remains unknown.

Top: With his old friend Dixie.

Bottom: Receiving his Millennium Giant award in 2000.

With typical bloody-mindedness Dave checked himself out of hospital to attend his eightieth birthday party in October 2009. Clockwise from top: With Derek Mountfield, Pat and Harry Ross; with Lord Granchester; with Pat; with Sir Philip Carter.

Dave Hickson's 80th Birthday
at
Club Everton (The Marquee)
on
Friday 30th October 2009
For 7.00pm - 8pm

RSVP Tel: 0151 677 5737   V.I.P.

Tickets: £60.00
Dress: Smart - Casual

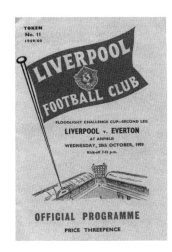

teammate, the winger Kevin Lewis, a fellow Portite whose father Hickson had played alongside as a boy with Ellesmere Port Town, were quitting football and going into business together.

Football was still subject to the maximum wage at the time and Hickson had previously spoken publicly about his concern in providing for his family after his football career. He had supplemented his salary at Anfield by working for a Liverpool clothing company and the partnership between him and Lewis was said to be an extension of the company's interests there.

Shankly said, 'Hickson and Lewis came to see me about this matter a few days ago. The Board were informed of their intention to leave football and to go into industry. There is nothing we can do. I'm sorry Lewis is taking this step because he is such a fine young player, and he is only 20. He has yet to come to his best as a player and his future was very bright.'

Shankly seemingly blamed Hickson for trying to drive the impressionable Lewis away from football and would ultimately keep Lewis on, offering him the highest possible wage available to Liverpool's first-team players at the time. When I spoke to Lewis about this article in March 2014, he said he remained incredulous about it and there was no truth whatsoever in him wanting to walk away from football to go into business.

Indeed, in the Liverpool Echo Michael Charters described the statement as a 'red herring', pointing to the fact that within a week of making it, Hickson was playing centre forward for Cambridge City in a 2–2 draw with Luton Town in the final of the Addenbrook Hospital Cup, a charity fixture, in which other league players wanted by Cambridge City took part.

With Football League clubs subject to the maximum wage (although only for a few more months), which restricted what they could pay their players, non-league clubs like Cambridge were free from such strictures. There was also no transfer fee for the non-league club to pay, unless they were elected to the Football League. 'They have an excellent ground, first-class dressing rooms, plenty of scope for improvement and extension of their stands and – best of all – they have a millionaire chairman, very keen on putting Cambridge on the football map,' wrote Charters.

Cambridge were owned at the time by a businessman called Harold Ridgon, whose interests encompassed butchers' stores, farming and the supply of building materials. Hickson was said to have been offered 'excellent terms for playing' as well as 'the choice of jobs in one of Mr Rigdon's many businesses' with a view to learning a trade when his career was over.

Dave, along with eleven other new players, was unveiled on 1 July 1961. The new signings included the former Tottenham and Irish international winger Johnny Gavin, the Sunderland left half Reg Pearce, and the Newcastle United goalkeeper, Brian Harvey. Hickson's overall package was said to be 'much higher than he could expect from any league club'. Asked at the time about his new team, Hickson replied: 'All I'll say is that I'm all right, Jack.' It seems extraordinary, but such was the way of English football in 1961.

After Liverpool I went to Cambridge City. Oscar Hold, who'd played alongside me as inside forward in my first days as an Everton player, called me and said, 'Come down here and play for me.' I could see that Shankly wanted Ian St John and Roger Hunt to continue at Liverpool and as always I just wanted to play football. I went down there and it was all right. I enjoyed it to a certain extent, but it wasn't the same. It was quite a jump going from a club like Liverpool challenging at the top of the Second Division to non-league. Again, I was staying in a hotel and not getting out much and I agreed to leave in December 1961.

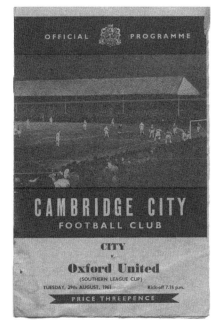

I returned to league football with Bury in January 1962 and at the end of the 1961/62 season came back to Merseyside with Tranmere Rovers. It meant that after the 1920s Scottish goalkeeper, Frank Mitchell, I became just the second man to play for all three Merseyside clubs.

Dave's Tranmere Rovers'
contract and (opposite)
with his new teammates.

Tranmere had been among the biggest spenders in lower leagues in this period, but it had not brought success. They had been relegated to the bottom tier in May 1961, and finished the following season fifteenth in the Fourth Division.

In December 1961 Tranmere appointed the former Bury manager Dave Russell as Walter Galbraith's successor. The Scot saw great potential in Merseyside's third team and would in time develop a prolific youth development system. He also wanted to develop a distinct identity from the two giants on the other side of the Mersey. Tranmere became exponents of Friday night football, as they tried to tap into the fan bases of Liverpool and Everton. Russell wanted Tranmere to stand out against the red of Liverpool and the blue of Everton, so they eschewed their traditional blue kit for an all-white kit (Leeds, in the same period, had done something similar in homage to the Real Madrid of Puskas and Di Stefano).

Dave had been listed by Bury for a fee of £1,000 and was initially signed on a two-month trial. However, he was injured in pre-season training and so didn't feature in any of the first six games. Of these matches Tranmere lost five, including a League Cup tie, and drew just one. Although he did not score on his debut against Hartlepools United on 8 September 1962 Dave's impact was dramatic: Tranmere won 6–1.

'The highlight was provided in the league debut of Hickson,' reported the Daily Post. 'Still not completely recovered from the troublesome thigh injury suffered in a practice game before the season's opening, he fashioned the home attack into a smooth working and thrustful machine. Hickson did not get his name on the score sheet, but that mattered little for he had a hand in creating no fewer than five of the Rovers' goals … Using the simple expedient of making deft flicks with his head and feet, Hickson exploited a gap in the middle leaving colleagues with clear-cut openings.'

The following Monday Hickson scored his first goal for Tranmere against Bradford at Prenton Park. On the Saturday he scored two and made a third as Tranmere ran out 3–2 winners at Darlington. Another brace followed in a Friday night game on 21 September in a 7–1 win over Southport.

We had some great times at Prenton Park. We didn't get out of the Fourth Division but we played some great games. In 1963, during the great freeze, we were drawn against Chelsea in the FA Cup. Most of the third round games were postponed because of the snow but we got all the supporters out with burners to keep the frost off because there was no undersoil heating then. Because of the fans' efforts we were one of the few ties to be played and featured on the TV highlights.

In the match at Prenton Park we led twice, but ended up drawing 2–2 and went to Stamford Bridge, where Chelsea took a two-goal lead. I made it 2–1 and we were plugging away for an equaliser when Terry Venables scored an unbelievable third goal. We had pushed them very close.

Footage of the first game, played at Prenton Park, shows Arctic-like conditions. It was a miracle that the game, played on 5 January 1963, took place at all. Neither Everton nor Liverpool played a home match for the best part of two months during this period. Although the markings are clear, the pitch is completely white. Hickson, ever the controversialist, is conspicuous by his presence, at one point grappling and punching an opponent, Graham Moore, at another arguing with the referee and attracting the opprobrium of the commentator. It was to be his last moment on the national stage.

As Dave Russell increasingly experimented with younger players, Dave was left on the sidelines for periods. Tranmere finished the 1962/63 season eighth, but Hickson was left out for the last five games as Russell invested his faith in youth.

They led the Fourth Division early in the 1963/64 season, but even on this stage, Dave's years were starting to take their toll. Reporting on Tranmere's August Bank Holiday win over York City, Michael Charters wrote, 'Hickson showed touches of his usual craft but now, of course, he lacks the speed to make any real impression on the game. The Hickson of three years ago would have been in position to score a couple of goals himself last night…'

In November 1963 Hickson was approached by Northern Irish club Ballymena to be their player-manager.

Number nine for Tranmere Rovers.

1965 in the Cheshire League Challenge Cup he caused the abandonment of an already tempestuous tie. The match had already been stopped after children were throwing fireworks towards the Macclesfield goalkeeper. Hickson had been booked too. Then with six minutes remaining and Ellesmere Port losing 2–0, he was ordered to leave the field by the referee, Mr Bennett of Altrincham. Ellesmere Port's chairman, Len Hill, then intervened, but Dave still did not see sense.

'The referee then walked off the field with his linesmen and when the crowd of nearly 2,000 realised that he had abandoned the match many of the spectators, mostly teenagers, rushed onto the pitch,' reported the Daily Post. 'There were angry demonstrations around the twenty-two players, who at that stage were uncertain what had happened. Scuffles broke out in two or three parts of the ground. Players were jostled as they tried to reach the dressing rooms and one man was seen to aim a blow at Glyn Ombler, the Port inside right.'

Hickson's crime had been 'persistent arguing'.

I came back to Ellesmere Port after my time in Northern Ireland. It was my home. My connections with Ellesmere Port Town, who I rejoined as a player, then player-manager, served me well. Most of the board were local councillors, so I got a job on the council with the public health board as a rat catcher. We had a van and we used to go around checking shops and offices for mice and all that.

Ellesmere Port Town went through several periods of dissolution and hopped between leagues throughout the 1970s. Dave returned as manager in 1976. His first love, however, remained on the other side of the Mersey.

Everywhere I went I still thought about Everton. They were the first result I looked for. But I never really went back to Goodison as a supporter. I was playing and then I was working.

'Ballymena feel that the Hickson personality will help their team,' reported the Liverpool Echo. 'His long experience in the game here is well known in Northern Ireland, and if he does join them it will be yet another unusual twist to this mercurial player's career.'

Dave would manage Ballymena for two spells, between November 1963 and December 1964, and again for four months from August 1967.

At Ballymena I took over from Geoff Twentyman as player-manager. It was mostly semi-professional, but we had five pros, including myself. We would train during the day and the rest came in by bus in the evenings. Then we'd all join up together on match days. I was probably a bit of a disciplinarian. I wanted players to do as I did, which was to give 110 per cent. I like Ballymena, it was a lovely place. We did quite well though. We finished third [they actually finished sixth], behind Linfield and Glentoran, who were really the big teams at the time. The second period I was there, my old Everton teammate Alex Parker took over from me and he ended up marrying a local girl.

After Ballymena, Hickson returned to Ellesmere Port Town, the place where it had all begun. His second debut on 30 January 1965 doubled their usual crowd to 1,102. 'The conditions were against a spectacular debut … for the ground was muddy on top and rock hard underneath,' reported the Daily Post. 'Hickson [was] content to trot around adding the odd touch of class.' His performance overall was considered 'subdued'.

He became player-manager later that year, but was still not averse to controversy. While playing Macclesfield Town on Saturday 11 September

Dave remained incredibly busy on and off the pitch through this time. He played exhibition matches regularly, in 1967 turning out against the Hungarian and Real Madrid legend, Ferenc Puskas, at South Liverpool FC. A year later he was to manage Puskas's great team-mate, Alfredo di Stefano, at the same venue, only for the Argentine to pull out at the last minute.

From the early-1980s he helped raise thousands playing for the charity team, the Over the Hill Mob, run by his friend Ivor Scholes.

On 21 March 1986, Dave married for the second time, to Pat at Christ Church, Port Sunlight, Wirral. The two would be inseparable for the rest of their lives, and Pat became a well-known and much-loved figure at both Goodison Park and charity functions. Every year, as soon as the football season was over, they would take long holidays together to Frejus in the south of France, usually for four or five weeks.

Memorandum of Ballymena United Football Club

An Agreement made this 5th day of May, 19.64

between BALLYMENA UNITED FOOTBALL CLUB, whose Grounds are situate in Ballymena, in the County of Antrim, hereinafter called the Club of the one part, and ....David...Hickson,..... (hereinafter called "the Player") of the other part.

1. The Club hereby agrees to engage the Player from the 15th day of August, 19.64, until the 30th day of April, 19.65 (both inclusive), for the purpose of Playing Football with the Club.

2. The Player hereby agrees to serve the Club for the purpose and period aforesaid, and not to engage himself to play football for any other person or Club during the said period.

3. In consideration of such service the Club hereby agrees to pay to the Player the sum of Twenty-five Pounds, per Week, from 15th August, 19.64 until 30th April, 19.65, except in Charity Matches, the amount paid to be pro rata to amount received from Charities Committee.

Provided always that the Player shall play in all Club Matches when required, and shall keep himself sober and in good playing form, and attend regularly to training and generally observe training instructions and do all that is deemed necessary to fit himself as an efficient football player.

4. Should any accident occur to the Player or he be in any way injured whilst at practice or play so as to incapacitate him from playing, the above sum shall continue to be paid; but should he be unable to play to the satisfaction of the Committee of the Club, through any cause other than the above named, payment will be withheld.

When unable to play through accident or injury a Doctor's Certificate **m u s t** be produced to that effect, and forwarded to the Secretary of the Club without delay.

As witness, the hands of the said Parties.

Name and Address of Witness :

For and on behalf of Ballymena United Football Club :

Secretary.

Player's Signature

Both Dave and Pat Hickson were generous supporters of North-west charities, notably the Lily Centre, the Everton Former Players Association and the Variety Club.

In the 1980s Dave was befriended by the former Coronation Street actor and theatre impresario Bill Kenwright, for whom he had been a boyhood hero. It would be one of the most enduring and important friendships of his life.

Kenwright would recall:

We played Liverpool for the first time at Wembley in the League Cup final in 1984. I was with my mum at home talking about getting a coach for all the family, red and blues who guided me through my life, the cousins, the uncles. I said to her, 'I would love Dave Hickson to come,' and she said, 'Ask him.' I said, 'I can't, he is Dave Hickson, he is God! I can't do it! I don't even know where he lives again!' It wasn't this day and age, but we got out the big Liverpool telephone directory and I went through it and there was Dave Hickson.

I dialled, and I was so frightened and nervous and the voice at the other end said, 'Hello.' I said, 'Mr Hickson?' 'Yeah!' 'My name is Bill Kenwright, and as you know we are playing the Reds at Wembley in 10 days, I wondered if you would come.' 'What you mean?' I said, 'I am taking my family down on a coach and I wonder if you would join us?' 'Can I bring Pat?' 'Of course you can,' [I didn't know who Pat was at the time] I said, 'bring who you like.'

He came and I spent time with him, and he just sat at the back of the coach, and he talked and he was grateful and gracious, but so quiet. The coach came into the Wembley car park, and this is one of my abiding Everton memories ... The coach stopped, and we all got out. Dave just got out with the rest of us. I swear to you, within 30 seconds there were hundreds of Evertonians around the coach, some of them picking up their kids and saying, 'Davey, he is David, he was named after you.' Dave was in shock, crying. We couldn't get to the entrance where we were sitting because they were there worshipping him. He didn't know. He truly did not know. He didn't wear a badge that said that 'I am humble'. He was shocked that people had that kind of emotion and that kind of love for him.

In 1989 Kenwright joined the Everton board. Five years later he lost out in a takeover battle for control of the club to the hamper millionaire, Peter Johnson, but remained a director and major shareholder. Kenwright used his influence to bring Dave back to the club.

I worked for the council until my 65th birthday, when I retired. Two days later I got a call from Bill Kenwright's office. 'How would you like to come home, son?' I'll never forget those words.

Dave with his Ballymena teammates.

Bill was an Everton director and wanted me to work on the PR side of the club. It was late 1994 and I'd been away from Goodison for almost exactly 35 years. Because I'd always been busy with work I hadn't been back to many games, but the club had never left me. As Alan Ball famously said, 'Once Everton touches you, nothing is ever the same,' and it never was with me.

I would work Monday, Wednesday and Friday and on match days – showing tour groups around Goodison, welcoming fans and visitors in the lounges, and helping with the club's public relations. I've been doing it for nearly 20 years now and I love it. It means everything to me.

Prior to Everton's 7–1 victory over Sunderland in November 2007, Dave suffered a major heart attack in one of the lounges at Goodison Park. He was rushed to hospital and on regaining consciousness was asked by nursing staff whether he expected to be playing in that fixture. Without missing a beat, he replied, 'Only in the last ten minutes.' Dave made a recovery from his heart attack, but at the age of 78 it finally put an end to his playing days with the Over the Hill Mob.

Everton's 1995 FA Cup win - with Dave a club employee again - was a happy day, with Dave appearing in the pre-match veterans game. Above, with Duncan Ferguson.

Everton is my family. I know each and every one of the people at the club. They've all been fantastic to me through my years there, first as a player and since I returned. I've had a few health problems in recent years and they have always been there for me. When I had my heart attack in 2007, Bill came to the hospital with me and stayed with me, despite a match going on at the same time. Another time I slipped and fell in the shower and ended up in hospital. The Reverend Harry Ross, who for many years ran St Luke's Church on the corner of Goodison, drove through the night from Blackpool to come and be with me at the hospital in Chester. It was fantastic.

If Everton was my family, to Pat and me the Kenwrights became like a second family. Bill had followed my career since he was a young lad on the terraces and I was the Everton number nine. He used to send me letters and I would write back to most of the children who wrote to me; all of them if I could do. Of course, I didn't know Bill at that time, but he used to say nice things about me and I'd post him a photo and quick reply. He seemed never to have forgotten that, because when I got to know him in the 1980s he still thought I was the best player he'd ever seen.

By then Bill had made his way in the world. He'd been an actor on Coronation Street and had become a very successful theatre impresario in London's West End. Out of the blue – 30 years since he'd sent me letters as a kid – he got in touch ahead of the Milk Cup final and asked if I'd like to join him as his guest at Wembley. What an experience that was! Ever since that time Bill has always been very kind to me, and I've been invited to join him in all sorts of places. He even invited Pat and me to New York for the opening night of Blood Brothers. We visited the Twin Towers and the Statue of Liberty as well and had a really lovely time.

My wife and I got to know all of Bill's family, and they were all great people. His mum, Hope, used to give us a call during the week and we'd have a chat and a catch-up. On Saturdays she'd join us at the games with Bill's brother Tommy. They are lovely people. When Hope passed away in July 2012, the funeral they conducted was some send-off. It was unbelievable, like a show; an absolutely fantastic way to say goodbye.

I love going to the games, but even now, in my eighties, I still feel like I'd like to get out there and have a run around.

One thing I can never understand is why a lot of players when they retire are so critical. I don't

David France
EVERTON HISTORIAN

Dave Hickson was a Blue brother. A refreshingly modest man who didn't like fuss. He once confessed to me: 'I wish I had been half the player that Bill Kenwright thinks that I was.'

My first glimpse of his signature quiff was on a bubble-gum card, the currency of playgrounds in the late 1950s and the portal to the world of football legends. Actually I stopped collecting them after an unfortunate incident involving him. Many years later, I told Dave my version of the facts was that I had found a sixpence and bought a half-dozen bubble-gum cards from the tuck shop opposite my junior school in the hope of snagging the card featuring Hickson. I soon overcame the disappointment of the number nine not appearing in my loot and sauntered home with six sticks of gum in my mouth and, by a sleight-of-hand, the sixpence in my pocket. Unfortunately, I bumped into my mother before I could dump my pickings. She frog-marched me back to the shop to return the coin and the cards and, most important, to apologise to the shop-owner. At most of our meetings, Dave reminded me that he and his magnificent coiffure had helped to make an honest man of me.

Dave was a swashbuckling centre forward who was often covered in blood, not always his own. But there was much more to him than being a gladiator. He was an ambassador. A man of integrity and dignity who was fond of all football fans on Merseyside, irrespective of allegiance. In all our years of friendship, I witnessed him lose his temper on only one occasion. Provoked by a Kopite in the Joe Mercer Suite, my old friend rocketed from mild-mannered man to pugilist in a nano-second. He was so angry. His facial muscles were taut. The blood vessels in his neck were raging. I could see the red mist in his eyes. With complete disregard for my own physical well-being, I stepped in between them. Before I could speak, Dave said: 'Go on, let me batter him.' At that point, we both roared with laughter as the mischievous Kopite slinked away. Dave was about 40 years older and 6 stone lighter than his opponent.

Back in 2011, Dave and I were lauded as Citizens of Honour at a ceremony at Liverpool Town Hall. As we followed the formal procession into the council chamber, he tapped me on the shoulder: 'Of all the people in Liverpool, they picked me and you – the two Blue Davids. Everyone knows what you've done but what did I do to deserve such an incredible honour?' My immediate response was: 'I think being the Cannonball Kid coupled with the fact that you made me an honest man are two good reasons.' Yes, he was more than a friend. He was a Blue brother.

And just in case you are interested. The secret to his mass of blond hair and signature quiff? Daily applications of bay rum.

Peggy O'Brien
CO-FOUNDER, THE LILY CENTRE

Dave Hickson was a patron of The Lily Centre, a breast cancer support centre based just off Scotland Road. Founded by Peggy O'Brien and her friend Winnie Keating, it is a drop-in centre that gives help to men and women affected by the disease. It is one of the two causes to which royalties from this book will be donated.

Dave and his lovely wife Pat attended most of our functions, if not all. Nothing was too much trouble for them. They were a lovely couple who are both sadly missed by us all at The Lily Centre. The support that they gave us was invaluable and Dave was a great ambassador, nothing was too much trouble. We have got a lot of good memories, which we will always treasure.

Dave with Peggy O'Brien (right) and Winnie Keating (left)

Dave and Pat used to love coming to our garden party every year. They always attended our black-tie dinner events, but Dave was so humble, he couldn't believe that all these people wanted autographs and a photo taken with him.

I remember when we put him up for the Citizen of Honour Award, and we kept it a secret from him, but whenever I was on the phone to Pat I would let her know what was happening. She was so excited about this award . . . Sadly Pat died on the day I received the call to confirm Dave was going to receive it.

In The Lily Centre Garden we have a plaque on the wall dedicated to these two lovely people. We've always admired Everton Football Club because they really did take care of Dave, and Bill Kenwright always looked after him too. We know because he told us, and it showed at his funeral. He was truly a one-off – they broke the mould when they made Dave Hickson.

Heswall & Neston Gingerbread Ladies Football Team

The stamps in Dave's passport reflect his end of season tours with Everton. Foreign travel to most of his generation of players in the 1950s was limited to national service and football tours.

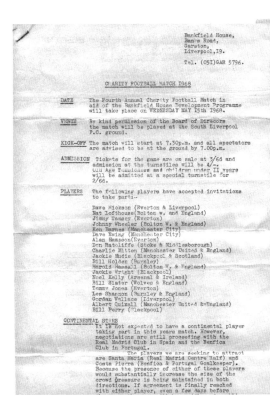

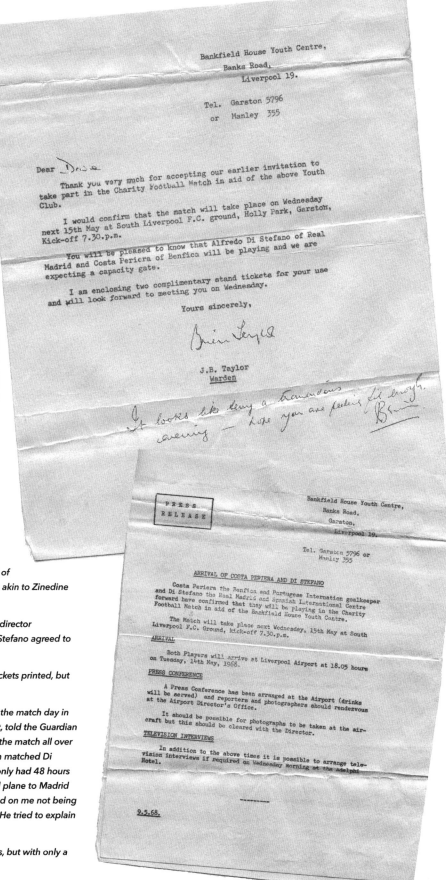

Dave's managerial career never rose above the heights of his brief spell in charge of Ballymena and his association with Ellesmere Port Town. However, in 1968, in a completely extraordinary encounter, he was set to manage one of the greatest players in football history: Real Madrid's five times European Cup winner, Alfredo di Stefano.

The match, which was to raise fund for Bankfield House Youth centre in Garston, followed a similar encounter a year earlier in which Hickson played alongside Ferenc Puskas, on a day when 10,000 people turned up. Puskas's appearance was a simple act of kindness towards an organisation he knew nothing about. It was akin to Zinedine Zidane rocking up to a community centre fundraiser in Kirkby.

Amazed by the power of football, a year later Bankfield House's director approached Pele, but when Santos turned down the request Di Stefano agreed to step in. Hickson was to be his captain and manager.

The match was advertised all over Liverpool, programmes and tickets printed, but 48 hours before kick off disaster struck.

'He agreed to come, but then there was a second telegram near the match day in which he said he couldn't,' Brian Taylor, who organised the event, told the Guardian in 2011. 'I was a bit disturbed about this because I'd advertised the match all over Liverpool and although we had two teams of stars, none of them matched Di Stefano's reputation. So as soon as I got the message – I think I only had 48 hours left before the game – I got on a plane to London, took a second plane to Madrid and got a taxi out to his house. The trouble was, I hadn't gambled on me not being able to speak Spanish and him not being able to speak English. He tried to explain to me, but to be honest I've no idea why to this day.'

Di Stefano tried to get a replacement from the Real Madrid ranks, but with only a reserve player on offer, Taylor declined.

Hickson's opportunity to manage a football immortal for the day had passed him by.

know why they do it. I was probably more dedicated than a lot of them but the thought has never occurred to me. I loved playing and I love supporting my club now, even when times are not so good. Of course, it's better when you're winning. When your team is playing good football and winning matches, it's a really lovely feeling.

In the last months of his life, as we worked together on the interviews that make up this book, Dave had several spells in hospital as his health worsened, but was always insistent on getting his fortnightly fix at Goodison, even when it seemed as if he wasn't well enough to go.

By July 2013 his health had deteriorated and on the morning of 8 July Dave's friend, Reverend Harry Ross, was called to the Countess of Chester Hospital.

He recalled: 'They told us he was very, very ill indeed; I got there at 11.30am and stayed until he passed away. I gave him the last rites and kept in touch with Bill Kenwright, told him what was happening. Bill kept texting me with all kinds of messages to pass on, even though Dave wasn't able to communicate. I just whispered in his ear what Bill was saying. I know how upset Bill was when we finally got in touch with him and said he'd passed away.'

At 2pm on 25 July 2013, the funeral of Dave Hickson was held at Liverpool's Anglican Cathedral. Hundreds of supporters lined the streets and applauded as his cortege passed Goodison Park. Everton's new manager Roberto Martinez and the entire Everton squad were in attendance for an emotional service, conducted by Reverend Ross.

Derek Temple
FORMER EVERTON TEAMMATE

Derek Temple played 274 times for Everton between 1956 and 1967 before moving to Preston North End. His finest hour came in the 1966 FA Cup final when he scored the winning goal in a 3–2 win over Sheffield Wednesday. In his early years in the first team Temple partnered Dave Hickson up front before moving out wide. He remains a popular and regular visitor to Goodison Park.

You partnered Dave for a short spell in 1957/58; what were your memories of that and what was it like to play alongside him?
Derek Temple: Dave was an old-fashioned centre forward. You could tackle from anywhere in those days, not like now where you can't tackle from behind. Then, as a forward you expected to be kicked up in the air as the ball was coming to you and your back was to goal, the defender was going to get you unless you were quick. But Dave didn't take to that very well. He used to get a bit upset and he used to lose his rag quite a lot. I always remember Dave, he used to go a little bit glassy-eyed when somebody kicked him and you'd be playing with ten men until he kicked the fella back.

He was a bit of a character, Dave, a good player though, a big strong lad. I made my debut as a centre forward but I didn't grow. Dave, as I said, was a big strong fella: he could take all the knocks. I played inside forward to him and I got quite a number of goals. He used to go in for balls and he'd hit everything and the ball would drop nicely for me a yard out and I was deadly from there! I got quite a number of goals from him.

What was it like when he left? Leaving for Liverpool . . .
DT: Well, I missed that because I went in the forces, I did national service. In '58 I went in the army and I was away. I ended up in Kenya, not fighting the Mau Mau but just at the end of the Mau Mau uprising, so I missed two years. When I think about it now it probably cost me an awful lot, that, because I was established in the first team and I might have gone on to better things, I think, with England and so on.

You and Dave both played under Johnny Carey. What was he like? How did he compare with Harry Catterick?
DT: I didn't like John Carey as a man. I didn't like him as a person but as a football man I thought his ideas were great. Harry Catterick was a lot deeper than John Carey. He came into Everton and he shook them up quite a bit, he made the defence strong. He used to say, 'Right, you're going out now and you've got a point, I don't want you coming back with less than a point.' Obviously he was very much geared up for clean sheets, he loved that, Harry. Although he was a centre forward in his playing days he had a very sound defence, which I think is fair enough – I think you have to have a good defence to win anything. He brought in a few players and he used to disappear up to Scotland and we didn't know where he'd disappear to at the time but then he'd come back with a player. And they were good players, very good.

What was it like when Dave was working for the club years after he'd left as a player?
DT: I used to see Dave occasionally. He loved Everton, he never wanted to leave. Then again, that's the thing about Everton, there are an awful lot of players, not local players like myself or Dave, but players from outside who fall in love with Everton and they support them for evermore. There's something about the club.

How popular was Dave in the later years when he was working at the club?
DT: Loved by a lot of people. The Cannonball Kid! He still had his big quiff, of course. Oh, he was popular, he did very well. He wasn't in the best of health for quite some time; he went very frail. He used to reminisce, his memory had gone a bit, and he'd give himself credit for goals he hadn't scored! But I suppose that happens to us all eventually!

Interview by George Gibson

'On the day of the funeral it was great to see the cathedral so packed,' recalled Reverend Ross. 'They were there for a legend. It had been a great privilege to know him and I am going to miss him so much.'

Bill Kenwright delivered a heartfelt eulogy in which he recalled a conversation he had recently had with Martinez, in which he was asked to explain his 'overwhelming love' for Everton.

I said, for me it's easy, just two words, Dave Hickson... That was the man who, for a lot of kids like me, post-war kids in Liverpool, frightened, a bit shy, timid, looking for a hero, we found one in Dave Hickson ...

Why? Couldn't have just been his quiff, though it was magnificent, the greatest blond quiff that you have seen in your life. Wouldn't have just been the goals, couldn't have just been that fact that he seems to be able to jump higher than anyone else and tackle more ... You cannot fool an Evertonian. They knew they saw in Dave Hickson something honest and something special.

For me, after I took two buses and a tram to get there, six, seven, eight years old, when you could go on your own in those days, he taught me how to dare. If he was there, when he walked out I felt 'I am fine'. They will go through a brick wall for me and for my team, and I am safe...

What I remember about the Manchester United game, the moment the whole game changed, was when he didn't come out for the second half. He came out three or four minutes later. He had liniment that was covered in blood, and it was the kind of gash that would be on the nine o'clock news today ... We were all looking at the touchline because we were just so desperate to have him back, and in one moment he took that liniment and threw it on the ground and the cheer was bigger than when he scored the winner, because he was back. He came on, he scored the winner and if he was partly in our history books, from that moment on he was forever in our history books.

Jack Dempsey once said, 'A true hero is someone who gets up when he can't.' Dave got up when he couldn't ...

He played hard, he played tough, but he played every ball as if his life, Evertonians' lives, depended on it.

Kenwright concluded the eulogy by reading out a poem by Paul Cookson, the poet in residence of the National Football Museum.

The Cannonball Kid has gone
But his memory and legacy live on

Swashbuckling cavalier
Fearless amongst the foe
A human battering ram
Boy's Own Hero

Unfailing courage
Left his head amongst the boots
Gave red for the blues
Boy's Own Hero

Those of us too young
Who never saw his bravery
Our dads said he was one of the best
Boy's Own Hero

Played for the team we wanted to play for
Played in the position we wanted to play
Played in the way we can only dream of
Boy's Own Hero

Nil Satis Nisi Optimum
Goodison Centurion and more
One hundred and eleven goals
Boy's Own Hero

Played for Liverpool, Tranmere too
But always blue and always true
Would have died for the Everton blue
Boy's Own Hero

The Cannonball Kid
Superstar, legend
A superman among men
Boy's Own Hero

But above all else, a gentleman
Modest, humble, down to earth
One of us, yet one of the gods
Boy's Own Hero

Dave Hickson
Our hero

Kenwright concluded: 'Dave Hickson, my hero. Joe Royle's hero. Ken Rogers' hero. The hero of tens of thousands of Evertonians, who are so grateful that we found him. God Bless You, Son!'

A few weeks later, some of Dave's ashes were interred at the side of the pitch at a private ceremony at Goodison Park and also at Pat's grave.

The Cannonball Kid had been reunited with his two great loves.

The Over the Hill Mob

BY IVOR SCHOLES

Dave Hickson lived and breathed football until his dying day. After he finished playing football for Ellesmere Port Town he continued to turn out in charity and exhibition matches until he was in his late seventies, notably for Billy Butler's Charity XI and for Ivor Scholes's famous team, Ivor's Over the Hill Mob. Over the course of more than two decades the Over the Hill Mob played more than 600 games and the aggregate age of the players in almost every match was more than 600 years. Dave made his last appearance for the Over the Hill Mob in October 2004.

I started watching my beloved Everton FC in 1952. I was called up for national service in 1957. Those five years remain the happiest of my football life. I was lucky to have watched my hero Dave Hickson in his pomp. What a centre forward! He had everything: speed, strength, two good feet, great header of the ball, and a toughness that had to be seen to be believed. The battles Dave had with the defenders of the day were X-certificate. Such gentleman as Higgins, Banks, Chilton, Allison, Chisholm, Malloy, White, Docherty, Ewing, Compton, Sillett, Harvey, Scouler, et al. made match days at Goodison Park gladiatorial. In fact when Peter Farrell led everyone out onto the pitch the tune played was 'Entry of the Gladiators' played by the band of the Grenadier Guards.

Dave Hickson's career has been well documented. However, 30 years after I last saw Dave play (in the 3–3 game with Manchester United a few months before the Munich air disaster) I was privileged to have him play for my veterans side, 'Ivor's Over the Hill Mob'.

Dave was 58 years of age when he made his debut for me versus Peter Hatt's Police Charity XI on 25 October 1987. I think he enjoyed himself – he stayed with my team for 17 years. Unbelievable!

Highlights of Dave's Charity Matches for Ivor's Over the Hill Mob

13 December 1987
The Brown House from Neston. Result 4–4, Dave scored two.

6 May 1989
Everton XI at Roby. Result 5–6. Raised money for the Hillsborough cause.
Guest players for Everton: Dave Hickson, George Telfer, Andy King, Roger Kenyon, Hughie McAuley, Billy Ashcroft, John Hurst and Brian Snagg.

26 November 1989
Rushen United, Isle of Man. Result 1–5. Attendance: 2,000. £3,000 raised for local charities.
Guest players for the match: Dave Hickson, Mick Lyons, Roger Kenyon, Gary Jones, Paul Power, Alan Whittle, Terry Darracott.
Man of the Match: Dave Hickson, aged 60.

24 October 1993
Royal Liverpool Philharmonic Orchestra. Result 12–4. DAVE HICKSON HAT-TRICK, also Man of the Match, aged 64.

13 November 1994
Bourne Arms. Result 7–2.
Probably the oldest front three in the history of football: Ivor Scholes, age 56; Dave Hickson, age 65, Eddie Hailwood, age 62.

30 May 1995
Bournemouth Sports. Final of the All-England Over-50s Veterans Cup at Macclesfield Town. Result 0–1.
Dave Hickson and other substitutes were prevented from appearing due to the organisers only allowing 20 minutes for the second half because the tournament was running late. A FARCE!
However, Dave was presented with a prize at Wembley for being the oldest player (aged 66) in the Umbro Cup in front of a 40,000 crowd, prior to the FA Vase final.

13 April 1997
Punjabi United. Result 6–0.
One of the Punjabi players kicked Dave during the match. Silly man. Dave told him off!

26 September 1999
Mynedd Isa Vets at Mold. Result 1–7.
Starring Joey Jones, ex-LFC. Big crowd at Mold Alexandra ground. Highlight of the game, our consolation goal by Dave Hickson with a diving header. Dave now 70 years of age.

10 October 2004
North Wales Select (Rhyl) at Colwyn Bay. Result 4–4.
Dave Hickson netted a penalty with ease. This match was his swan song, aged 75 years.

Over the Hill Mob Playing Record 1985–2007

Played	Won	Drawn	Lost	For	Against
618	263	94	260	2034	1951

Everton in the 1950s

The 1950s were Everton's hard times, a period when the club's standing has never been so low. The golden generations that preceded and followed this decade sandwiched a generation of players that tried hard, but collectively failed to live up to Everton's Nil Satis Nisi Optimum mantra, fulfilled by the likes of Mercer, Lawton, Young, Harvey, Kendall and Ball. Failure on the pitch sometimes descended into humiliation: relegation in 1951, the club's lowest ever league place in 1953 (sixteenth in the Second Division), its record defeat in 1958 (10–4 at Tottenham) and various other on-pitch massacres (8–2 v. Newcastle and Huddersfield, 6–0 at relegated Sheffield Wednesday, 6–1 at home to Arsenal). In September 1958 Dixie Dean told Granada TV that this was 'the worst Everton team I have ever seen' and that it needed 'about half a dozen new players'.

Yet the 1950s was also a period of unprecedented high attendances, great hope and periods of high drama. Matches such as the 1953 FA Cup win over Manchester United have been written into Goodison lore. There were brushes with glory, including two FA Cup semi-final appearances. Some of the most distinguished players in the club's history pulled on a blue shirt during this period: Ted Sagar, Bobby Collins, Derek Temple and, of course, the Cannonball Kid himself.

For the first part of the decade, the club were managed by Cliff Britton. Described by Dean as 'one of the finest half backs in the history of the game', Britton shared a quarter-century-long association with Everton as player and manager. As a 1930s player Britton had won the FA Cup, Second Division title and England honours with the club. After the war Britton turned to management with Burnley and proved to be one of the most outstanding young bosses in football. In his first season he won promotion from the Second Division and took Burnley to

the FA Cup final, which they lost to Charlton Athletic. A year later he led Burnley to third place in the First Division.

Everton, by contrast, had suffered disaster after disaster in the post-war era. Theo Kelly was manager, but the club's former secretary was an administrator first and foremost and had no aptitude for or experience of dealing with players. Everton had haemorrhaged their best players from the great pre-war team, mostly as a result of Kelly's lack of man-management skills. This included Lawton and Mercer, while T.G. Jones was ostracised. The board of directors, meanwhile, interfered in team affairs with disastrous effect. In early September 1948 they were involved in a flurry of activity, making Albert Juliussen – one of the worst acquisitions in

the club's history – a record signing, and selling Jock Dodds – one of the few players to rise above the mediocrity of the post-war years. They carried these dealings out while actively searching for a 'professional manager', rather than waiting to see if the new man actually sanctioned them.

Their appointment was Britton, which, given his experience at Everton as a player and the outstanding potential shown at Turf Moor, seemed the correct one. The new manager was soon aware of the scale of the task facing him at Goodison. A minute from a board meeting on 8 November 1948 noted: 'Mr Britton detailed his opinions of the playing personnel, on which only two or three seemed to be of the required First Division calibre.' Britton detailed some targets and the board gave him a massive budget to acquire players.

He was allowed to approach Middlesbrough's Wilf Mannion, a brilliant inside forward who shone for club and country. But his failure to buy him for Everton highlighted the difficulties in signing players during this era. Mannion was on a highly publicised strike at the time and desperate to leave Ayresome Park; he hadn't played for Middlesbrough in months and any right-minded chairman would have been desperate to sell him. But despite Britton bidding a British record £25,000 for him, Middlesbrough would not sell Mannion. A £16,000 offer to buy the Arsenal wing half Alex Forbes met a similar rebuttal; likewise Liverpool's Cyril Done and Wolves' Johnny Hancocks.

Instead Britton was forced to look at players from places like Doncaster, Rotherham and Ireland, where Everton visited on an end of season tour. It was a difficult situation, but Everton's scouting system – with directors dispatched to watch players – was antiquated compared to that which Matt Busby was instituting at Manchester United.

There were predictably dismal consequences on the pitch. Everton finished 1948/49 eighteenth, and in the same position the following year, when relegation was only averted in their final game of the season. There seemed to be a sense of lingering complacency that permeated the club. In September 1950, Ranger, the *Liverpool Echo's* football correspondent, issued the following warning:

Today the position of Everton is as precarious as it was at this time last season and in the absence of a quick and decisive improvement, it may soon be almost as desperate as it was two years ago. Not to mince matters, it must be abundantly clear now to all connected with the club that the present side is nowhere near good enough. I have refrained in the past few weeks from unduly stressing its weaknesses. In an effort to back Mr. Britton's endeavours to put more confidence and spirit into the players I have avoided adverse criticism as much as possible hoping that some satisfactory solution might be found.

I have felt for some time that Everton's long-term policy of producing their own young material, admirable though it is, is not the one best suited to their immediate requirements. Undoubtedly they have a few promising young players, and T.E. Jones, Hickson, McNamara, and one or two others may make the top grade in due course, while O'Neill, Moore, and to a slightly lesser degree Clinton have already proved their worth. But the time to blood young players is when the team is winning not struggling. Everton's great need at the moment is three or four first class men of experience who can come into the side at once and make their presence felt by football of the finest vintage. In short, something like we had in the old days from Dean, Cliff Britton himself, Lawton, Coulter, Stevenson, Mercer, Tommy Jones, and a host of others whose memory only makes today's comparisons bitter when we think of how low the club has sunk ...'

Jimmy Harris
FORMER TEAM MATE

Jimmy Harris was a versatile forward who played across the Everton forward line in the second half of the 1950s. He both partnered Dave Hickson, as a winger and inside forward, and served as his replacement at centre forward. Harris's 72 goals in 207 Everton appearances, make him equal 25th – with Duncan Ferguson – in Everton's list of all-time goalscorers. He later went on to enjoy success with Birmingham City, winning the League Cup and appearing in the Inter City Fairs Cup final.

I was thrown into the team in the 1955/56 season and did exceptionally well. Dave was sold to Aston Villa early on in the season and I took his place at centre forward. Did I feel the pressure as a rookie taking on Dave's berth? I don't think Dave was doing much at the time. I think he was built up to be something I didn't think he was. I thought he scored most of his goals in the Second Division, from 1951 to 1954, where the game was more suited to the old type of centre forward.

It was true that he was a different person on the pitch to how he was off it. He did lose it on the pitch. Not many people come out with the actual facts of his behaviour on the pitch, but it was not very good. He was a bully at Goodison, but when we went away the opposition were all waiting for him, and we'd get it dished out there. There were not many people that could get him to calm down. I think Cliff Britton could a bit, but they couldn't do anything on the pitch.

Cliff Britton was very strict as a manager. A bit dour. He would be there at Bellefield but you would never see him in a tracksuit; he always had his trilby on, and his coat; he just looked the part. Managers didn't come down the touchline in those days; they did it all from the stands and then came down to the dressing room at half-time.

The club was hopeless after Britton left. Ian Buchan was manager but the directors ran it. I got a bad hamstring injury in one match and had to stay on for over 60 minutes with it. I hardly played much that season. That's how ignorant they were. Imagine players now staying on an hour with a hamstring injury.

The directors made such a balls of it that I think we lost a bit of interest too. They played me at Old Trafford in the FA Cup, and I'd been in hospital for an injection in that hamstring. I told them I wasn't fit, but where was I at three o'clock on Saturday afternoon but in the centre circle at Old Trafford! I didn't get a kick. And when I got back on the coach as I went past the directors, Major Jack Sharp I think it was, said, 'He didn't do much today, did he!'

When Dave returned in 1957 the club was in such disarray. I went on the right wing for two seasons, where I was getting plenty of goals and was playing all right. The man who made a difference was Bobby Collins, of course. He was the one that sorted the club out. How we stayed up before then, I don't know. I suppose it was only that we could win home games against just about anybody that we stayed up.

We had the talent at Everton during the 1950s. There was a lot of talent at Goodison: Brian Harris, myself, Derek Temple, Mick Meagan. Mick was there all that time and we were bringing left backs in from anywhere. It felt unbelievable the way things were run. I scored 21 in my first season. Next season it was Jimmy Glazzard, who came from Huddersfield to play centre forward. Alan Shackleton, Peter Harburn were all signed. These fellows running the club didn't seem to respect us, the ones who could do it. I mean, some of the teams that were put out in 1956/57 season were unbelievable. Fellows coming in who hadn't played before. We'd never heard of some of them then, and never heard of them since!

John Willie Parker
HICKSON'S PARTNER IN CRIME

John Willie Parker scored 89 goals for Everton in 176 appearances. A small and deceptively casual goal-poacher, he formed a lethal partnership with Dave Hickson, helping John Willie to become the club's leading scorer four seasons in a row from 1951 until 1955. John Willie died in 1988, but here Arthur Parker tells the story of his brother – whom he knew as 'Billy'.

Our Billy was the nicest fella you've ever met in your life. His attitude to football was that it's better than working on the docks. He started playing football during the war when he was in his teens. He was too young to get in the army but he wouldn't have got in the army anyway because he had a kidney out when he was 14. Having a kidney out then was a lot different than having a kidney out now and nobody thought he'd ever play football again, but he said he would and he did.

He travelled for five years from our place in Birkenhead over to Everton, where he played as an amateur. They used to pick him up for the A, B and C teams at Lime Street and he'd go and they'd play at Bootle Stadium. It's where they built Tate and Lyle's.

He got into the first team and he couldn't go wrong in the Second Division. He was leading goalscorer in the three seasons they had in the Second Division and when he came up to the First Division he scored seven goals in the first three games, I think. He never got excited, he was the coolest man in the world. That's the way he was.

In 1953 Everton got to the FA Cup semi-final where they played Bolton. They were in with a great chance, but funny things happened. Jimmy O'Neill used to have a black cap in his goalkeeper's bag with his gloves and stuff, and he lost that beforehand. He was a bag of rags, our Billy said. Hickson was told by Britton to stay away from Malcolm Barrass, who was a big fat centre half for Bolton who kicked everything that moved. In the first 10 minutes, Hickson said something to Barrass and the next thing he's on the floor and suffering from concussion. There were no subs then so (and it wouldn't have been allowed now) they let him play on. But Dave didn't know where he was. Even when he came off he thought they'd won, but they got beat 4–3 as you know.

Our Billy's biggest mates were the Irish lads, Peter Farrell, Tommy Eglington, George Cummins, Jimmy O'Neill; they didn't half get on well. We only had a two-bedroomed house in Birkenhead and they all used to come to our house for their dinner, and me Mam used to give them egg and chips! Outside there was a big school playground and they'd go on at half-four, put their gear on and play the school kids, and they'd be diving all over the place! They were crackers, it was brilliant, absolutely brilliant.

He finished at Everton in 1956 and went to Bury, him and Jock Lindsay. Jock used to play at left back, but he had a bad leg break and him and our Billy went to Bury for a £7,000 joint fee. Their manager Dave Russell later asked him to move to Tranmere, but he never got on with Russell and left the game. Although he courted a girl called Olive for about 30 years, Billy never married: he lived in the family home all his life, him and our brother Lawrence; two bachelors.

After football, as most of them did, he went into the pub trade with Threlfalls. He managed a pub but he could never hold a licence because in them days you had to be married to hold a licence. He ran a lot of pubs, as did a lot of Everton players. As a matter of fact he got an invite off Everton to go and watch the 1966 Cup final, and then he got a letter off Threlfalls saying he couldn't go because Eddie Wainwright was sick and he needed to manage the pub. Eddie Wainwright went to Wembley!

It was a brilliant club and I played for a few local clubs but I would have loved to have played in that side, not for winning anything or anything like that but just to have been in amongst them; you know the times they used to have and the things they used to do, like kids sometimes, but they were brilliant.

In November 1950 the board gave Britton a 'unanimous vote of confidence' but things did not improve. By the last day of the season Everton needed to travel to Sheffield Wednesday – who were already virtually assured of relegation – knowing a point would see them survive. With their destiny in their own hands, Everton dismally capitulated, losing 6–0. '1-2-3-4-5-6 … OUT!' ran the *Liverpool Echo* headline, continuing: 'Everton run into a Goal "Blitz".' Everton finished bottom with Wednesday, also relegated, a place ahead of them.

Britton had been in charge for nearly three years at this point, with ample time – even given the difficulties in the transfer market – to make his own impression on the team. But a month into the 1951/52 season, he blithely announced to the board that his team was not good enough to gain promotion and that he should be allowed to pursue a policy of giving youth players a chance. It was at this stage that Dave Hickson and Tony McNamara joined their contemporary, the centre back T.E. Jones, in the first team.

However, Everton muddled along in the wrong part of the Second Division for too long. In October 1951 Ranger wrote that 'the prestige of [Everton] today is lower than ever before, and that unless something is done quickly you are going to have difficulty keeping out of the Third Division'. He warned of derby matches 'against Tranmere Rovers, Southport and Chester at Goodison Park next season. It is no joke. It is a tragic possibility.'

The board and manager refused the implorations to spend big to help Everton out of the mire. On the eve of the 1952/53 season, the chairman Ernest Green said, 'Everton is determined, as far as possible, to keep out of

the transfer market, and to build up our teams from the junior ranks, trained and coached by the club staff.' This was not what supporters wanted to hear.

Everton would finish the 1951/52 season seventh and 1952/53 sixteenth – the worst two league positions in the club's history. Only an FA Cup semi-final appearance in March 1953 – following the Hickson-inspired run – alleviated a dire situation for Evertonians.

Remarkably, despite his failures, in September 1953 Britton was made general manager and given a new contract worth £2,650 per year, plus a large house in Thornton and a car. When he finally won promotion back to the First Division, he was given a bonus of £2,000 for getting Everton out of a predicament he had put them in. These were significant amounts at a time when players were earning around £15 per week.

Everton unquestionably had talented players, such as the Irish duo Peter Farrell and Tommy Eglington and the forward pairing of Hickson and his partner in crime John Willie Parker. They would score 56 league goals between them in the season that Everton went up. Reflecting on that campaign, Dave always ascribed Everton's success to the spirit that was inculcated in the dressing room, a sense of shared responsibility among the players. Never really a critical person, Dave was vaguely dismissive of Britton's role in the promotion.

Everton's captain backed up Dave's view. 'It was certainly the greatest moment of my life and I knew from the look of the lads in the bath after the game that they were experiencing the same emotion,' said Farrell. 'You can take it from me that no captain could have the honour of being skipper

Gerry Moore
EVERTONIAN AND TRUSTEE EFPF

Gerry Moore is a lifelong Evertonian who has followed the Blues throughout the entire postwar era. Now in his seventies, he is a trustee of the Everton Former Players Foundation.

I used to have a saying that if Dave came off the pitch without being covered in bandages, covered in blood, he'd never had a game. That was Dave; and yet when he walked off the pitch you wouldn't believe it was the same man. He was a unique character in my eyes; probably one of the nicest men I've ever met. My wife is not into football but she's met him on numerous occasions; she thought he was a lovely, lovely man, and really was warm to him. But when he walked out on the football pitch it was a case of, 'I might have been nice to you yesterday, but out of the way.' But that was the way football was played in those days; it was blood and guts and blood and thunder.

He had no fear at all. If it was a bus coming towards him and Dave thought 'I can get the ball', Dave would tackle the bus, as simple as that. He wanted that ball; he wanted to win at any cost, even if it meant upsetting a teammate. I don't think that's a bad thing; I think there's too little of that today. I often watch the modern games and say, 'Where's the sentiment?' You see a player miss an open goal and he just laughs. That wasn't Dave; Dave had to win at any cost.

Today if there's a spot of blood on a player's shirt they're off. In those days it would run down his shirt, he'd be wiping his forehead or his cut with the shirt. I never found the aggression wrong but I think it used to wind the fans up and they used to love it and say, 'Go on, Dave, go on; chase him, chase him, tackle him; well done, Dave.' I think in the modern game, when you watch games, crowds still love a trier. Has that ever changed? I don't think it has.

The crowds were much bigger in the 1940s and 1950s. Goodison, when there were 77,000, 76,000 people there, was unbelievable. It was absolutely unbelievable. Health and Safety wasn't involved in those days – it was a case of get down there as soon as you could, get in the queue. On this one occasion I'll always remember you could not walk down Bullens Road; you were just shoulder to shoulder, face to face. You just couldn't get through. We had to try and find the end of a queue, if you could find one. People would shout, 'Where are you going?' 'Hey, there's a queue here, mate.' And you'd realise the end of the queue was right down the other end. That's how it was.

On this particular day my father was getting concerned because I couldn't move. Somebody saw me and said, 'Get that kid out of there.' I was only a schoolboy and I remember being picked up and they carried me on my back, over their shoulders, straight through the turnstile and dropped me on the other side to wait for my father to get in. They were concerned I was going to get crushed, hurt.

But to get seventy-odd thousand was just tremendous. The noise was deafening. I can visualise it now. You couldn't talk, you couldn't hear the other person. If you tried to speak to the guy two or three places from you there was no way he could hear you. It was just unbelievable.

On the field, I think the rules were so different in those days. The referees allowed a lot more to go on. Because in those days I don't think they were assessed as they are today. If you're a referee and I'm an assessor you know that if you make a mistake I'm going to watch you, probably call you to one side and say, 'Why did you do that?' They're looking after their own job and their own back as well. I think in those days they let a little bit more go on. I don't mean they would allow a deliberate leg-break; that was never in the game. If it happened, unfortunately it happened; but it wasn't done like a criminal or a yobbo doing it.

I think Dave just played the game with his heart on his sleeve. He loved it; his teammates loved him. I know they said on the pitch he could be an absolute swine, but you just had to love him; he was a lovely fellow, a loveable rogue. And that to me was Dave.

to a better crowd of lads. The fact that Everton are now back where they belong in Division One can be attributed in no small way to the team spirit of the boys that made it possible. Whatever our faults, and irrespective of whether we played well or badly, one thing predominated over everything else, namely, that in every game during the season we were all pals both on and off the field.'

There were, however, brief signs that Britton's long-term view might reap dividends in the 1954/55 season – Everton's first back in the First Division and Dave's initial taste of top-flight football. In March 1955, Everton moved up to fourth place, just four points behind league leaders Chelsea and with three games in hand. Ultimately Everton's lack of quality showed through: instead of emerging as title challengers, they won just one of their last ten games and finished eleventh.

Britton's faith in youth would precipitate Hickson's departure early in the 1955/56 season. Unimpressed at being dropped in favour of the hitherto untried Jimmy Harris, he asked for and got a transfer to Aston Villa.

Britton's time in the Goodison hot seat came to a messy end in February 1956. As the directors planned a five-week, ten-game end of season tour of the United States they decided to appoint H.R. Pickering, a longstanding member of the backroom staff, acting manager in Britton's absence – but without telling Britton first.

On hearing the news Britton was furious and, after taking legal advice, claimed Everton were in breach of contract. He claimed two years' salary as compensation and the termination of his contract. A panicked board agreed to rescind the offer to Pickering and wrote Britton a grovelling letter stating that they possessed 'a collective desire to remove any sense of grievance which you may entertain, however misconceived it may be'.

Britton was not assuaged by the attempts at reconciliation. He attended an emergency board meeting at which further attempts were made to smooth the ill feeling. Instead Britton exploded into a rage, threatening that he 'could ruin the reputation of every director'. According to a later statement by the board (and backed up by a copy of the document he presented to them) he said that the only way he would stay was if the board paid for a 40-year lease on his house. When this was rejected, Britton stormed out of the meeting, calling the directors 'despicable men'.

Everton's chairman, Ernest Green, was dispatched to calm him. He told Britton the view of Everton's legal counsel that his walkout represented a breach of contract not by Everton, but by him. Britton responded that he sought no further part in the management of the club – and so ended his seven-and-a-half-year reign at Goodison. His demands for compensation were seemingly never met.

Britton later managed Preston North End and Hull City. 'He was obviously power mad,' recalled Tom Finney, who was his star player at Deepdale, the sort of footballing genius Britton never got to manage for Everton. 'I didn't care for him and couldn't tolerate the ridiculously over-strict and unsympathetic way in which he dealt with players … Cliff just didn't know how to ease off and it led to some almighty rows.'

The appointment of Loughborough University PT lecturer Ian Buchan as Britton's replacement in May 1956 seemed at once a highly progressive and strange move by the Everton board. A man at the

DAVE HICKSON | THE CANNONBALL KID

DAVE HICKSON | THE CANNONBALL KID

forefront of sports science, the board recognised the changing face of football and the growing emphasis on physical conditioning. And yet he came with no experience of professional football. It was never quite clear how much overall say Buchan ever had over team selection and there was no upswing in performance during his 28-month spell as 'Head Coach'. Everton finished the 1956/57 season fifteenth and the 1957/58 campaign sixteenth, progressing no further than the fifth round of the FA Cup in 1957 and the fourth a year later.

Dave had returned from Huddersfield for a cut-price fee in the summer of 1957, but the focus was still largely on youth. Derek Temple, Brian Harris and Brian Labone all made breakthroughs during this period and would serve Everton well through their subsequent 1960s golden era.

It was at this time that the financial influence of the millionaire Littlewoods Pools magnate, John Moores, began to be felt by Everton. Moores had first taken a shareholding in the club during the war years, but in 1957 he loaned funds for floodlights, and over the summer of the following year he nudged the perennially frugal board to open the club's coffers. Their first major signings in years were the Falkirk duo, Eddie O'Hara and Alex Parker, and they were joined by Brighton's centre forward, Peter Harburn, for whom Dave was meant to give way at the start of the 1958/59 season. This time Dave stood firm and did not ask for a transfer. Instead, fans did the talking for him and angry letters piled into the local press as Everton lost their first six games.

'It is perfectly obvious that there is something wrong at Goodison. Despite the accent on youth they have produced nothing worth bragging about. When Mr Buchan came to Goodison he was quoted as saying that Everton were playing a negative type of football. I don't know what he calls the type they're dishing up now. If it were any more negative it would be non-existent,' wrote T. Bartley of Little Crosby. 'We have read about weight-lifting but never anything about heading, trapping and passing the ball in which the team are so poor. They are also slow to make up their minds in going for the ball and also moving into open spaces for a pass,' complained R.J. Darwin of Aughton. Even the chairman Dick Searle waded in, claiming: 'Everton are three yards slower than opponents they have met this season.'

After years of inertia, the board finally made some dramatic changes. Buchan was sacked and replaced by Johnny Carey, the former Manchester United captain turned Blackburn Rovers manager. Celtic's Bobby Collins – one of the greatest players of his generation – was signed for £24,000. After taking over in October 1958, Carey steadied the listing Everton ship. Relegation was comfortably averted and a thrilling brand of football

instituted. Everton finished the 1958/59 season having scored 71 goals. They also conceded 87 and finished sixteenth.

However, there was no miraculous transformation. Everton started the 1959/60 season slowly, not winning a game until the seventh fixture of the season when the Cannonball Kid – who else? – struck a brace against Blackburn Rovers. The mutterings of discontent became a chorus a month later when Hickson was sold to Liverpool to accommodate the Leeds forward Alan Shackleton in the centre-forward berth. Even half a century later the pain at the Cannonball Kid's departure was still felt by a generation of Everton fans.

Everton ended the 1950s in seventeenth place after a 4–0 defeat at Manchester City. The result – and the fact that they had beaten the same team 2–1 at Goodison 48 hours earlier – seemed to typify the decade.

Three straight league defeats in January 1960 put Everton in real danger of relegation again. But the Moores money, largely squandered previously, began to be spent wisely. Over the course of 1960 Carey added Roy Vernon, Tommy Ring, Jimmy Gabriel, Billy Bingham and Alex Young to the Everton squad. Everton finished the 1960/61 season in fifth place – their highest post-war position.

It was not, however, enough for the great taskmaster John Moores, by now chairman. He sacked Carey near the end of the season and replaced him with the Sheffield Wednesday manager, Harry Catterick, who had started the 1950s as Everton centre forward and was the man the Cannonball Kid had replaced in 1951. Everton had come full circle. Their hard times had ended and a golden era was about to begin.

James Corbett

Fan Memories

A SELECTION OF STORIES ABOUT HOW DAVE IS REMEMBERED BY FANS

My grandfather used to talk about Dave whenever the Blues came up in conversation.

It's fair to say he idolised him, even to the extent of having similar haircuts! They both came from the same era, where men were not only men, but gentlemen too.

I had the honour of being the best man at my friend's wedding at Goodison Park. When we spotted Dave lurking outside the suite in which the ceremony was taking place we asked him to come in. Dave had time for everyone, posed for photos and even took the bride and groom on an unofficial tour!

But my favourite memory of him was the vice-like handshake he gave me that day, very similar to the one my late grandfather would have given.

If Dave was my grandfather's hero, he must have been one hell of a man.

Ian O'Callaghan, Skelmersdale

I am a lifelong Evertonian who started watching the Blues back in the 1960s and was a season-ticket holder for more than 20 years before moving to France in 1990. Not too long after moving here I met Dave and was a friend of his and his wife Pat until their sad deaths.

I spoke to Dave on many occasions about players and Shankly and he always got me tickets for matches when I was back home.

The first time I met Dave it was through a friend, as he was staying with a group of friends in some of the mobile homes in Holiday Green, Frejus, and I was working in the site next door.

My friend, Ade, called me to say he had a group of Evertonians staying with him. He had mentioned me and they said they had some magazines about the club they would pass on to me (the Evertonian etc.). He added that one of them said he had played for Everton and his name was Dave Hickson. 'Have you heard of him?'

'God, yes, he's a legend of the 1950s!' I said.

When Dave heard there was a mad Evertonian working next door he said he would call in and say hello. First, however, I met up with Ade later that day and he passed me the magazines.

The next day I was going to work and took them with me when I heard a voice a bit behind me. 'That bloke's got a copy of the Evertonian.' I turned around and saw this group of men and in the middle was Dave, instantly recognisable with his quiff. He said, 'Hello, you're Mike.'

At that moment I wished I could have told my dad that I had met Dave Hickson and he knew who I was. It is only a small story, but to me still very moving.

Mike Thompson, France

Sometime in the late 1990s I was playing veterans' football for Wirral Vets and we played against a team from Liverpool called Plesseys. In this game I was in goal and noticed the ex-Everton player John Bailey playing at left back. I was then told that Dave Hickson was playing up front. Halfway through the second half Bailey crossed the ball to Dave, who headed it with some power for his age towards goal. What a dilemma. Do I try and save it . . .? No chance! I watched with admiration as it flew into the top of the net. He still had it.

Steve Barrell, Wirral

I was fortunate enough to meet Dave around September 2007 during a tour of Goodison. My very first introduction was the 1989 BBC History of Everton video that I used to watch constantly as a young lad, where I first heard, 'I'd break any bone in my body for any club I play for but I'd die for Everton.' I was quite excited to find out that Dave took the tours. I got to the ground and almost as soon as I reached it Dave extended his hand and asked, 'Are you Deian?' He pronounced my name correctly, which for someone like me whose name is always being pronounced wrongly was a brilliant first impression.

The tour itself was fantastic. I managed to get a photo of Dave and an autograph which is still very much a prized possession of mine, tucked as it is inside said case of the BBC history video. The absolute highlight for me and one which will stay with me till my dying day was seeing Dave at the edge of the Goodison turf with a faraway twinkle in his eye as he reminisced in his mind's eye about his playing days. That alone was worth the tour admission.

Deian Lye-Vella, Bath

I met Dave Hickson after the 2009 FA Cup final. I was leaving after a great but disappointing experience and bumped into him in the Club Wembley area. I only wanted to say hello and maybe get a photograph, but he engaged me in conversation about how we had played and how far we had come as a team. He made no indication of wanting to get away and his beloved wife stood there patiently as she must have done so many times in her life. He chatted to me for a good 10 minutes and I felt as if I had known him all my life. My two lads stood there open-mouthed as an Everton legend stood talking to their dad like an old friend. A priceless moment in my life.

John Kenny, Wallasey

I grew up idolising Dave Hickson. My dad had a budgie that he sat up a lot of nights with when we had gone to bed, training it to speak a specific phrase – 'Good old Dave Hickson, dirty Billy Liddell'. So you have to be of a certain age to appreciate that!

My dad had a season ticket in the Bullens Road stand. Up until about age eight, he used to take me to the games on his own ticket. He used to go through the same gate every game and got to know the gate man. So he used to slip him a pack of 10 cigarettes, throw me over the gate and then up into the stands. Not everyone could make the games so there was usually a spare seat going close by.

One night, I don't remember who we played, but the stand was quite empty. Anyway, the game got going but there was a bit of a buzz around where we sat. Wondering what it was all about, we turned around and there was Dave sitting about three rows behind. To me it was like seeing God! I think I spent more time sneaking a peek behind me than watching the game!

At half-time I asked my dad if I could ask him for his autograph. So, programme in hand, I went up and asked him to sign it. Needless to say, I didn't sleep much that night and took my programme into school next day to show only the Blues supporters in my class – and there were a lot of them at that time.

I've lived in Canada for the last 40 years and still follow everything that is Blue.

John Hands, Toronto, Canada

Dave Hickson was my dad's favourite player, he told me all about him when I was a boy. I was born in 1974 and did not get a chance to see him play. My brother and I are both Blue to the core, but due to our parents moving me from Merseyside to Hong Kong when I was young, we didn't get the chance to visit Goodison much. I went once when I was back in England on holiday when I was about 10, but my brother, who was born in Hong Kong, had never had the pleasure.

After we returned to England, my brother and I decided to make the pilgrimage to Goodison for a home match against Fulham. We were both living down South at the time, so we made a weekend of it.

The game was great, Leon Osman scored in the last few seconds to make it 2–1, so happy days, we headed off to the Winslow for a few beers. The Everton music was playing and we had

made friends with some middle-aged Blues, who didn't care that we sounded like southerners and were a lot younger than them, and we were having a great time, when I looked over and in walked Dave Hickson. I was awestruck. I nudged one of the guys we were with and said, 'That is Dave Hickson!' He kind of just nodded and said, 'Yes, he's a great guy, he's always here after games.' I was just staring at him as he came in, stayed for about a minute and walked back out, getting many a pat on the back as he left. I kept saying, 'I can't believe I just saw Dave Hickson!'

Then the guy I had nudged, realising that this was quite a big deal to someone like me, who rarely gets a chance to attend the match, said, 'Do you want to meet him? I know him.'

Naturally I said yes and we both got up, moved to the door and he shouted, 'Dave!' Mr Hickson turned round and said, 'Hello, Corky.' (I think that was his name.)

'This lad wants to meet you,' he said. Dave came over and shook my hand. I remember he had the strongest vice-like grip. I think I just looked at him and muttered something like 'Honour to meet you, sir'. He asked if I had enjoyed the game, I said yes. Then he looked at me and said, 'We are on our way now, lad.' I agreed, Everton were starting to play some good stuff with Arteta and Cahill.

Then that was it, he was off. I went in, sat down with a massive smile on my face, had a great night out and could not get over the fact that I had met my old man's hero.

Andrew Oxton, Liphook

I am now a 70-year-old man, but in 1973 when I was 29/30, I worked for a small engineering company in Ellesmere Port (maybe 30 employees). The manager of this company was a good friend of Dave Hickson, and when a football match was suggested between our company and that of another (perhaps Lever Brothers), a team was formed to play on one of the football pitches in Bromborough – on the left of the New Chester Road heading south, opposite Bromborough Village – after work one evening. We were told that Davie boy would 'turn out' for us, and would play centre forward! I personally played at inside left and 'schemed' for Davie!

Before the game, we were in the changing room, and directly opposite me, sitting changing, was Davie. I said to him, 'Oh Dave, if only my friends could see me now, sitting in the same changing room with you.' He just smiled!

After the game started, Dave became aware that our right winger was wearing 'trainers' – not boots – and was slipping all over the place on the grass. Dave was very irate, continually getting annoyed at the very idea! At another stage of the game, while I paused with the ball looking to make a pass, I was 'dropped' by a tackle from behind – quite heavily! The same individual, shortly after, tried to rough up Davie while jumping for the ball, but Dave just 'dropped' him – no outrage or comments – just brushed him off!

I can't remember the final score or who won, but here was an old Everton great who must have been in his forties then, turning out on a weekday evening to play with our team – a load of amateurs – and enjoying every minute.

John F.

Dave Hickson was part of my boyhood football education despite me being a Blackburn Rovers fan. He was that kind of player you wanted in your team and whenever Dave was playing against your team you knew you were in for a tough afternoon. He was every centre half's nightmare.

I remember one game in particular at Ewood Park where Dave and Rovers' centre half Matt Woods (ironically, a former Everton player) had been having a rare old tussle all afternoon. After one particular incident – I think Dave made one tackle too many – Matt lost his patience and retaliated and was sent off, a rare occurrence in those days. Rovers fans were so incensed they sent a petition to the FA asking for the sending-off to be rescinded. To this day I don't know the outcome. Dave, I'm sure, left Ewood that day with that cheeky grin.

Dave Hickson was the quintessential centre forward who loved the game and played it accordingly.

Fred Cumpstey, Blackburn

It was 10 years ago that I met Dave Hickson. Julio, from the Valparaiso restaurant, had asked if I would take two Chilean lads on the Goodison Park tour. Thus, on that Friday we were there waiting, a mixed crew, all ages, at least four nationalities including Malaysian and German, and a group from Northern Ireland.

It was our pleasure to discover that the tour guide was none other than Dave Hickson, known to some as the Cannonball Kid, to others not at all, but present to all with his amazing quiff and serene features. He couldn't have been better, a mine of information, full of little anecdotes, attentive to all and ever patient with pauses while I translated for the chilenos. And at the end he made us all a cuppa. Dave Hickson made us a cup of tea! Typical of his unassuming nature.

He, for his part, was delighted to be there, happy to have been given a place back in Goodison by the club and in particular by Bill Kenwright. I asked him if he would like to come to the Ruleteros Society [the Everton de Vina del Mar supporters club] dinner the following Wednesday. Delighted, he said, but would we mind if his wife Pat came along? Did we mind?!

And so began a friendship with the Ruleteros. Pat and Dave turned up bright and early, no dramatic entrance for them, and spoke to everyone that night, happy to be there and happy to hear of our Chilean links. Anything to promote Everton. Pat was Dave's unofficial secretary, remembering stuff he had temporarily forgotten and delighted rather than irritated that so many wanted a piece of Dave, a photo, a quote or simple recognition. Not for the first time were they labelled 'Posh and Hicks', in the nicest possible slant. That night he accepted the position of Honorary Life Patron. Over the years, Dave and Pat attended many of our dinners as well as the Shareholders' Dinner in 2009 which celebrated the Chilean centenary and the Everton links. On more than one occasion he was serenaded by the 'Davie Hickson/ Davy Crockett' song.

Dave, in his capacity as tour guide, supported our trip to Chile in 2005 and pointed us in the direction of some surplus Everton kit, which we took out to help Chilean youngsters and amateur teams. He and Pat always asked after us and, at the Shareholders' Dinner, Pat organised the presentation of crystal decanters, a gift to the Chile Everton Board, accepted on their behalf by Julio Arellano, the aforementioned manager of the Valparaiso and Chilean consul. And at that amazing Everton v. Everton game in August 2010 they were both there, chuffed to bits like the rest of us. It was with great sadness later that year that we learned of the passing away of Pat, Dave's soul mate.

It was, of course, a crushing blow to Dave but he soldiered on and, typically, as well as maintaining his regular attendance at Goodison, was determined to fulfil engagements and commitments, helped in no small measure by Julia and Derek Mountfield and his 'chauffeur and drinking pal' Barney. At the 2013 Ruleteros Dinner, one of celebration for Chile Everton's recent promotion, Dave was there, happily signing, posing, reminiscing and, indeed, competing. He it was who won a bottle of wine in Gerry's quiz and took his prize with consummate satisfaction. He raised a glass to us and we in turn, and in common with all Evertonians and others, raise one to him. En el corazón, Dave, in our hearts, forever. Gracias por todo. Thanks for everything.

Tony Heslop, Crosby

My dad was a great admirer of Dave Hickson and one incident involving the whole family sticks in my mind. We were living in Bolton at the time and back in November 1992, as a birthday treat, we booked a tour of Goodison followed by a family meal up in the restaurant. For reasons involving traffic en route, we were late, parked our car and dashed along Goodison Road (where my mum was born in 1918) to the club entrance. We thought we had messed things up. But no, not a bother, Dave Hickson, who I recognised right away, was waiting at the door (he was looking after visitors/guests that day) with an encouraging smile on his face and that great quiff of his. 'You must be the Humphreys' family,' he said.

'Yes,' we said breathlessly!'

'Well,' he said, 'don't worry, we would never start without you.' The kids glowed. A calm and true gentleman.

Peter Humphreys, Dublin

My memories are of the sterling work Dave did behind the scenes on match days, although never before he made sure his wife was okay and sat comfortably. On one occasion Danny Cadamarteri had been voted man of the match having scored a winner against Liverpool. Dave brought Danny to our table and asked if we would like a photo alongside Danny. I asked Dave if he would join us on the photo. He replied that he would, 'If it's okay with Danny'. I was of a mind to say that Danny was not fit to lace Dave's boots, but after such a display of courtesy I declined.

John Griffiths, Wallasey

My dad, Peter O'Hare, was involved in a charity football match up in Prescot. The man running things was Brian Snagg, manager of the local Fusilier pub. 'Snaggy' always ran charity games and sportsman's evenings – and, although every one was usually a success, Brian had a reputation for being disorganised.

Don't get me wrong, things got done. There was just an almighty panic on the day or night.

This was a Sunday afternoon in early summer and we all turned up at Prescot Cables FC to play against some legends . . . and spotted a pair of rugby posts! Brian hadn't realised the rugby season was in full flow and so we kicked off with high crossbars on our minds! Particularly me, as (being the youngest) I was told to go in goal! A teenager – underneath 10-foot-high posts!

I was made to feel better by some of the company I'd be keeping on the pitch – including the legendary Dave Hickson. Glimpsed only through my Grandad Mac's stories and the Official History of Everton video ('I'd die for this club . . .'), Dave was larger than life. That hair was in full flow . . . and he had on his boots from back in the day. You know the type: high ankles, tough leather and caked in mud. Brilliant!

Then it happened. An innocuous passage of play ended when the ball – slightly more contemporary than Dave's boots – landed at Hickson's feet. Twenty-five yards from goal, he flicked it up and volleyed on the half-turn. I never smelled it! True, it might have sailed over in a normal goal (!), but I don't think so.

Dave Hickson had slotted a beauty past me and I couldn't be happier. After the game – The Cannonball Kid played the full 90 minutes – we shook hands and I thanked him. His grace, humility and class stayed with me and continue to do so. It also gave me the opportunity to go straight to my nan's for Sunday dinner and tell my grandad all about it.

The stuff dreams are made of. Well, rugby posts aside …

Alan O'Hare, Wavertree

I was outside Upton Park in 1953 when Everton were due to play West Ham in a Second Division game. I was working in London at the time and had gone to the ground with my landlady's nephew. We watched the team coach come in and Davy got off with a plaster over one of his eyes from an injury. He spotted me with my Everton scarf on and asked me and my mate whether we had tickets. On hearing that we didn't he took us into the Everton dressing room and went round the players until he managed to get two spare tickets. He gave them to the two of us and told us to go and enjoy the game. It was a real genuine act of kindness from someone who didn't even need to stop to talk to us, let alone go out of his way to get us tickets.

I watched the game and the final score was 3–1 to West Ham. The next time I saw Davy was when we took a tour of Goodison with my own children about seven years ago. Then I was able to tell him about that day in 1953 and how much it had meant to me. Davy was as perfect a gentleman during that tour as he had been back in 1953.

I'm 90 this year and loved Davy Hickson and have never forgotten that day at Upton Park and the generosity of a 'star'.

Tom Bell, Wallasey

Statistics

DAVE HICKSON'S PROFESSIONAL PLAYING CAREER

EVERTON
APPEARANCES 243
GOALS 111

ASTON VILLA
APPEARANCES 12 GOALS 1

HUDDERSFIELD TOWN
APPEARANCES 54 GOALS 28

LIVERPOOL

APPEARANCES 67
GOALS 38

BURY

APPEARANCES 8 GOALS 0

TRANMERE ROVERS

APPEARANCES 45 GOALS 21

EVERTON

1951-1952

Date			Competition	Venue	Opponents	Result		Goals
Sat	1	Sep	Div 2	A	Leeds United	2	1	
Wed	5	Sep	Div 2	H	Nottingham Forest	1	0	
Sat	8	Sep	Div 2	H	Rotherham United	3	3	⚽
Wed	12	Sep	Div 2	A	Nottingham Forest	0	2	
Sat	27	Oct	Div 2	A	Luton Town	1	1	
Sat	3	Nov	Div 2	H	Bury	2	2	
Sat	10	Nov	Div 2	A	Swansea Town	2	0	
Sat	17	Nov	Div 2	H	Coventry City	4	1	⚽⚽
Sat	24	Nov	Div 2	A	West Ham United	3	3	⚽
Sat	1	Dec	Div 2	H	Sheffield United	1	0	
Sat	8	Dec	Div 2	A	Barnsley	0	1	
Sat	15	Dec	Div 2	H	Southampton	3	0	⚽⚽
Sat	22	Dec	Div 2	A	Sheffield Wednesday	0	4	
Tue	25	Dec	Div 2	A	Doncaster Rovers	1	3	
Wed	26	Dec	Div 2	H	Doncaster Rovers	1	1	⚽
Sat	29	Dec	Div 2	H	Leeds United	2	0	
Sat	5	Jan	Div 2	A	Rotherham United	1	1	⚽
Sat	12	Jan	FAC 3	A	Leyton Orient	0	0	
Wed	16	Jan	FAC 3 Rep	H	Leyton Orient	1	3	
Sat	19	Jan	Div 2	H	Cardiff City	3	0	⚽
Sat	26	Jan	Div 2	A	Birmingham City	2	1	⚽⚽
Sat	9	Feb	Div 2	H	Leicester City	2	0	⚽
Sat	16	Feb	Div 2	A	Blackburn Rovers	0	1	
Sat	1	Mar	Div 2	H	Queens Park Rangers	3	0	
Sat	8	Mar	Div 2	A	Notts County	0	0	
Sat	15	Mar	Div 2	H	Luton Town	1	3	
Sat	29	Mar	Div 2	H	Swansea Town	2	1	
Sat	5	Apr	Div 2	A	Coventry City	1	2	
Fri	11	Apr	Div 2	H	Hull City	5	0	⚽
Sat	12	Apr	Div 2	H	West Ham United	2	0	⚽
Mon	14	Apr	Div 2	A	Hull City	0	1	
Sat	19	Apr	Div 2	A	Sheffield United	2	1	
Sat	26	Apr	Div 2	H	Barnsley	1	1	

EVERTON

1952-1953

Date			Competition	Venue	Opponents	Result		Goals
Sat	23	Aug	Div 2	H	Hull City	0	2	
Mon	25	Aug	Div 2	A	Sheffield United	0	1	
Sat	30	Aug	Div 2	A	Blackburn Rovers	1	3	
Wed	3	Sep	Div 2	H	Sheffield United	0	0	
Sat	6	Sep	Div 2	H	Nottingham Forest	3	0	
Wed	10	Sep	Div 2	A	Barnsley	3	2	⚽
Sat	13	Sep	Div 2	A	Southampton	1	1	
Sat	4	Oct	Div 2	A	Swansea Town	2	2	⚽⚽
Sat	25	Oct	Div 2	H	West Ham United	2	0	
Sat	1	Nov	Div 2	A	Fulham	0	3	
Sat	13	Dec	Div 2	A	Bury	5	0	
Sat	20	Dec	Div 2	A	Hull City	0	1	
Sat	10	Jan	FAC 3	H	Ipswich Town	3	2	⚽⚽
Sat	17	Jan	Div 2	A	Nottingham Forest	3	3	
Sat	24	Jan	Div 2	H	Southampton	2	2	
Sat	31	Jan	FAC 4	H	Nottingham Forest	4	1	
Sat	7	Feb	Div 2	H	Brentford	5	0	⚽⚽⚽
Sat	14	Feb	FAC 5	H	Manchester United	2	1	⚽
Sat	21	Feb	Div 2	H	Swansea Town	0	0	
Sat	28	Feb	FAC QF	A	Aston Villa	1	0	⚽
Sat	7	Mar	Div 2	H	Leicester City	2	2	⚽
Sat	21	Mar	FAC SF	Maine Rd	Bolton Wanderers	3	4	
Wed	25	Mar	Div 2	H	Fulham	3	3	
Sat	28	Mar	Div 2	A	Rotherham United	2	2	⚽
Sat	4	Apr	Div 2	H	Plymouth Argyle	2	0	
Mon	6	Apr	Div 2	H	Huddersfield Town	2	1	
Tue	7	Apr	Div 2	A	Huddersfield Town	2	8	⚽⚽
Sat	11	Apr	Div 2	A	Leeds United	0	2	
Wed	15	Apr	Div 2	H	Bury	3	0	⚽
Sat	18	Apr	Div 2	H	Luton Town	1	1	
Wed	22	Apr	Div 2	H	Lincoln City	0	3	
Sat	25	Apr	Div 2	A	Birmingham City	2	4	⚽

EVERTON

1953-1954

Date			Competition	Venue	Opponents	Result		Goals
Wed	19	Aug	Div 2	A	Nottingham Forest	3	3	
Sat	22	Aug	Div 2	A	Luton Town	1	1	
Mon	24	Aug	Div 2	A	Hull City	3	1	⚽
Sat	29	Aug	Div 2	H	Oldham Athletic	3	1	
Wed	2	Sep	Div 2	H	Hull City	2	0	
Thu	10	Sep	Div 2	A	Notts County	2	0	
Sat	12	Sep	Div 2	H	Doncaster Rovers	4	1	
Sat	19	Sep	Div 2	A	Blackburn Rovers	0	0	
Wed	23	Sep	Div 2	H	Notts County	3	2	⚽⚽
Sat	26	Sep	Div 2	H	Derby County	3	2	
Sat	3	Oct	Div 2	A	Brentford	0	1	
Sat	10	Oct	Div 2	A	Plymouth Argyle	0	4	
Sat	17	Oct	Div 2	H	Swansea Town	2	2	
Sat	24	Oct	Div 2	A	Rotherham United	2	1	⚽
Sat	31	Oct	Div 2	H	Leicester City	1	2	
Sat	7	Nov	Div 2	A	Stoke City	4	2	⚽⚽⚽
Sat	14	Nov	Div 2	H	Fulham	2	2	⚽
Sat	28	Nov	Div 2	H	Leeds United	2	1	⚽
Sat	5	Dec	Div 2	A	Birmingham City	1	5	
Sat	12	Dec	Div 2	H	Nottingham Forest	3	3	⚽⚽
Sat	19	Dec	Div 2	H	Luton Town	2	1	
Fri	25	Dec	Div 2	H	Bristol Rovers	4	0	⚽⚽
Mon	28	Dec	Div 2	A	Bristol Rovers	0	0	
Sat	9	Jan	FAC 3	H	Notts County	2	1	⚽
Sat	16	Jan	Div 2	H	Bury	0	0	
Sat	23	Jan	Div 2	A	Doncaster Rovers	2	2	⚽
Sat	30	Jan	FAC 4	H	Swansea Town	3	0	⚽
Sat	6	Feb	Div 2	H	Blackburn Rovers	1	1	⚽
Sat	13	Feb	Div 2	A	Derby County	6	2	⚽
Sat	20	Feb	FAC 5	A	Sheffield Wednesday	1	3	⚽
Wed	24	Feb	Div 2	H	Brentford	6	1	⚽⚽
Sat	27	Feb	Div 2	H	Plymouth Argyle	8	4	⚽⚽
Sat	6	Mar	Div 2	A	Swansea Town	2	0	⚽
Sat	13	Mar	Div 2	H	Rotherham United	3	0	
Sat	20	Mar	Div 2	A	Leicester City	2	2	⚽⚽
Sat	27	Mar	Div 2	H	West Ham United	1	2	
Sat	3	Apr	Div 2	A	Leeds United	1	3	
Sat	10	Apr	Div 2	H	Stoke City	1	1	
Fri	16	Apr	Div 2	H	Lincoln City	3	1	
Sat	17	Apr	Div 2	A	Fulham	0	0	
Mon	19	Apr	Div 2	A	Lincoln City	1	1	
Sat	24	Apr	Div 2	H	Birmingham City	1	0	⚽
Thu	29	Apr	Div 2	A	Oldham Athletic	4	0	⚽

EVERTON

1954-1955

Date			Competition	Venue	Opponents	Result		Goals
Sat	21	Aug	Div 1	A	Sheffield United	5	2	
Wed	25	Aug	Div 1	H	Arsenal	1	0	
Sat	28	Aug	Div 1	H	Preston North End	1	0	
Tue	31	Aug	Div 1	A	Arsenal	0	2	
Sat	4	Sep	Div 1	A	Burnley	2	0	
Wed	8	Sep	Div 1	H	West Bromwich Albion	1	2	
Sat	11	Sep	Div 1	H	Leicester City	2	2	⚽
Wed	15	Sep	Div 1	A	West Bromwich Albion	3	3	⚽
Sat	18	Sep	Div 1	A	Chelsea	2	0	
Sat	25	Sep	Div 1	H	Cardiff City	1	1	
Sat	2	Oct	Div 1	A	Manchester City	0	1	
Sat	9	Oct	Div 1	A	Aston Villa	2	0	⚽
Sat	16	Oct	Div 1	H	Sunderland	1	0	
Sat	23	Oct	Div 1	A	Huddersfield Town	1	2	⚽
Sat	30	Oct	Div 1	H	Manchester United	4	2	⚽
Sat	6	Nov	Div 1	A	Portsmouth	0	5	
Sat	13	Nov	Div 1	H	Blackpool	0	1	
Sat	20	Nov	Div 1	A	Charlton Athletic	0	5	
Sat	27	Nov	Div 1	H	Bolton Wanderers	0	0	
Sat	4	Dec	Div 1	A	Tottenham Hotspur	3	1	
Sat	11	Dec	Div 1	H	Sheffield Wednesday	3	1	⚽
Sat	18	Dec	Div 1	H	Sheffield United	2	3	
Sat	25	Dec	Div 1	A	Wolves	3	1	⚽⚽
Mon	27	Dec	Div 1	H	Wolves	3	2	
Sat	1	Jan	Div 1	A	Preston North End	0	0	
Sat	8	Jan	FAC 3	H	Southend United	3	1	⚽
Sat	15	Jan	Div 1	H	Burnley	1	1	
Sat	29	Jan	FAC 4	H	Liverpool	0	4	
Sat	5	Feb	Div 1	H	Chelsea	1	1	
Wed	23	Feb	Div 1	H	Manchester City	1	0	⚽
Sat	5	Mar	Div 1	A	Sheffield Wednesday	2	2	
Sat	19	Mar	Div 1	A	Manchester United	2	1	
Wed	23	Mar	Div 1	H	Huddersfield Town	4	0	⚽
Sat	26	Mar	Div 1	H	Portsmouth	2	3	
Sat	2	Apr	Div 1	A	Blackpool	0	4	
Fri	8	Apr	Div 1	H	Newcastle United	1	2	
Sat	16	Apr	Div 1	A	Bolton Wanderers	0	2	
Wed	20	Apr	Div 1	A	Leicester City	2	2	⚽
Sat	23	Apr	Div 1	H	Charlton Athletic	2	2	
Sat	30	Apr	Div 1	A	Sunderland	0	3	
Wed	4	May	Div 1	H	Aston Villa	0	1	

EVERTON

1955-1956

Date			Competition	Venue	Opponents	Result		Goals
Sat	20	Aug	Div 1	H	Preston North End	0	4	
Wed	24	Aug	Div 1	A	West Bromwich Albion	0	2	

ASTON VILLA

Mon	5	Sep	Div 1	H	Birmingham City	0	0	
Sat	10	Sep	Div 1	H	Blackpool	1	1	
Sat	17	Sep	Div 1	A	Chelsea	0	0	
Wed	21	Sep	Div 1	A	Birmingham City	2	2	
Sat	24	Sep	Div 1	H	Bolton Wanderers	0	2	
Sat	1	Oct	Div 1	A	Arsenal	0	1	
Sat	8	Oct	Div 1	A	West Bromwich Albion	0	1	
Sat	15	Oct	Div 1	H	Manchester United	4	4	⚽
Sat	22	Oct	Div 1	A	Everton	1	2	
Sat	29	Oct	Div 1	H	Newcastle United	3	0	
Sat	5	Nov	Div 1	A	Burnley	0	2	
Sat	12	Nov	Div 1	H	Luton Town	1	0	

HUDDERSFIELD TOWN

Sat	26	Nov	Div 1	H	West Bromwich Albion	1	0	
Sat	3	Dec	Div 1	A	Charlton Athletic	1	4	
Sat	10	Dec	Div 1	H	Tottenham Hotspur	1	0	
Sat	17	Dec	Div 1	A	Portsmouth	2	5	
Sat	24	Dec	Div 1	H	Sunderland	4	0	
Mon	26	Dec	Div 1	A	Blackpool	2	4	⚽
Tue	27	Dec	Div 1	H	Blackpool	3	1	
Sat	31	Dec	Div 1	A	Aston Villa	0	3	
Mon	2	Jan	Div 1	A	Bolton Wanderers	2	2	
Wed	11	Jan	FAC 3	A	Bolton Wanderers	0	3	
Sat	14	Jan	Div 1	H	Wolves	1	3	
Sat	21	Jan	Div 1	A	Manchester City	0	1	
Sat	4	Feb	Div 1	H	Cardiff City	1	2	
Sat	11	Feb	Div 1	A	Preston North End	2	1	⚽⚽
Sat	18	Feb	Div 1	H	Burnley	1	0	
Sat	25	Feb	Div 1	A	Luton Town	2	1	
Wed	7	Mar	Div 1	H	Birmingham City	1	1	
Sat	10	Mar	Div 1	A	Sheffield United	1	3	
Sat	17	Mar	Div 1	H	Everton	1	0	⚽
Sat	24	Mar	Div 1	A	Newcastle United	1	1	
Sat	31	Mar	Div 1	H	Manchester United	0	2	
Mon	2	Apr	Div 1	A	Arsenal	0	2	
Tue	3	Apr	Div 1	H	Arsenal	0	1	
Sat	7	Apr	Div 1	A	West Bromwich Albion	2	1	⚽
Sat	14	Apr	Div 1	H	Charlton Athletic	4	0	⚽
Sat	21	Apr	Div 1	A	Tottenham Hotspur	2	1	⚽
Sat	28	Apr	Div 1	H	Bolton Wanderers	3	1	⚽⚽

HUDDERSFIELD TOWN   1956-1957

Date			Competition	Venue	Opponents	Result		Goals	
Sat	24	Nov	Div 2	A	Rotherham United	3	3	⚽	1
Sat	1	Dec	Div 2	H	Blackburn Rovers	0	2		
Sat	15	Dec	Div 2	H	Liverpool	0	3		
Mon	24	Dec	Div 2	A	Notts County	2	1		
Wed	26	Dec	Div 2	H	Notts County	3	0	⚽	1
Sat	29	Dec	Div 2	H	Fulham	1	1	⚽	1
Sat	5	Jan	FAC3	H	Sheffield United	0	0		
Mon	7	Jan	FAC3 R	A	Sheffield United	1	1 (aet)		
Mon	14	Jan	FAC3 2R	N	Sheffield United	2	1	⚽	1
Sat	19	Jan	Div 2	A	Grimsby Town	2	1		
Sat	26	Jan	FAC 4	H	Peterborough United	3	1	⚽	1
Sat	2	Feb	Div 2	H	Doncaster Rovers	0	1		
Sat	9	Feb	Div 2	A	Stoke City	1	5	⚽	1
Sat	16	Feb	FAC 5	H	Burnley	1	2	⚽	1
Mon	22	Apr	Div 2	A	Middlesbrough	2	7	⚽	1

EVERTON

1957-1958

Date			Competition	Venue	Opponents	Result		Goals
Sat	24	Aug	Div 1	H	Wolves	1	0	
Wed	28	Aug	Div 1	A	Manchester United	0	3	
Sat	31	Aug	Div 1	A	Aston Villa	1	0	
Wed	4	Sep	Div 1	H	Manchester United	3	3	
Sat	7	Sep	Div 1	H	Chelsea	3	0	⊗
Tue	10	Sep	Div 1	A	Arsenal	3	2	⊗
Sat	14	Sep	Div 1	H	Sunderland	3	1	⊗⊗
Sat	21	Sep	Div 1	A	Luton Town	1	0	
Sat	5	Oct	Div 1	A	Leicester City	2	2	⊗
Sat	12	Oct	Div 1	A	Newcastle United	3	2	⊗
Wed	16	Oct	Div 1	H	Arsenal	2	2	
Sat	19	Oct	Div 1	H	Burnley	1	1	
Sat	26	Oct	Div 1	A	Preston North End	1	3	
Sat	2	Nov	Div 1	H	West Bromwich Albion	1	1	
Sat	9	Nov	Div 1	A	Tottenham Hotspur	1	3	
Sat	16	Nov	Div 1	H	Birmingham City	0	2	
Wed	20	Nov	Div 1	H	Blackpool	0	0	
Sat	23	Nov	Div 1	A	Portsmouth	2	3	
Sat	30	Nov	Div 1	H	Sheffield Wednesday	1	1	
Sat	7	Dec	Div 1	A	Manchester City	2	6	
Wed	25	Dec	Div 1	H	Bolton Wanderers	1	1	
Thu	26	Dec	Div 1	A	Bolton Wanderers	5	1	⊗
Sat	28	Dec	Div 1	H	Aston Villa	1	2	
Sat	4	Jan	FAC 3	A	Sunderland	2	2	⊗⊗
Wed	8	Jan	FAC 3 Rep	H	Sunderland	3	1	⊗
Sat	11	Jan	Div 1	A	Chelsea	1	3	
Sat	15	Feb	Div 1	H	Leicester City	2	2	
Sat	22	Feb	Div 1	H	Newcastle United	1	2	
Sat	1	Mar	Div 1	A	Burnley	2	0	
Sat	8	Mar	Div 1	H	Preston North End	4	2	
Sat	15	Mar	Div 1	A	West Bromwich Albion	0	4	
Sat	22	Mar	Div 1	H	Portsmouth	4	2	
Sat	29	Mar	Div 1	A	Birmingham City	1	2	
Sat	5	Apr	Div 1	H	Tottenham Hotspur	3	4	⊗⊗
Mon	7	Apr	Div 1	A	Leeds United	0	1	
Sat	12	Apr	Div 1	A	Sheffield Wednesday	1	2	
Sat	19	Apr	Div 1	H	Manchester City	2	5	

EVERTON

1958-1959

Date			Competition	Venue	Opponents	Result		Goals
Mon	1	Sep	Div 1	A	Preston North End	1	3	
Sat	6	Sep	Div 1	H	Arsenal	1	6	
Tue	9	Sep	Div 1	A	Burnley	1	3	⊕
Sat	13	Sep	Div 1	A	Manchester City	3	1	
Wed	17	Sep	Div 1	H	Burnley	1	2	
Sat	20	Sep	Div 1	H	Leeds United	3	2	
Sat	27	Sep	Div 1	A	West Bromwich Albion	3	2	⊕⊕
Sat	4	Oct	Div 1	H	Birmingham City	3	1	⊕⊕
Sat	11	Oct	Div 1	A	Tottenham Hotspur	4	10	
Sat	18	Oct	Div 1	H	Manchester United	3	2	
Sat	25	Oct	Div 1	A	Blackpool	1	1	
Sat	1	Nov	Div 1	H	Blackburn Rovers	2	2	⊕
Sat	8	Nov	Div 1	A	Aston Villa	4	2	
Sat	15	Nov	Div 1	H	West Ham United	2	2	
Sat	22	Nov	Div 1	A	Nottingham Forest	1	2	
Sat	29	Nov	Div 1	H	Chelsea	3	1	⊕⊕
Sat	6	Dec	Div 1	A	Wolves	0	1	
Sat	13	Dec	Div 1	H	Portsmouth	2	1	
Sat	20	Dec	Div 1	H	Leicester City	0	1	
Fri	26	Dec	Div 1	H	Bolton Wanderers	1	0	⊕
Sat	27	Dec	Div 1	A	Bolton Wanderers	3	0	⊕
Sat	3	Jan	Div 1	A	Newcastle United	0	4	
Sat	10	Jan	FAC 3	H	Sunderland	4	0	⊕⊕
Sat	17	Jan	Div 1	A	Arsenal	1	3	
Sat	24	Jan	FAC 4	A	Charlton Athletic	2	2	
Wed	28	Jan	FAC 4 Rep	H	Charlton Athletic	4	1 (aet)	⊕⊕
Sat	31	Jan	Div 1	H	Manchester City	3	1	⊕
Sat	7	Feb	Div 1	A	Leeds United	0	1	
Sat	14	Feb	FAC 5	H	Aston Villa	1	4	⊕
Wed	18	Feb	Div 1	H	West Bromwich Albion	3	3	⊕
Sat	21	Feb	Div 1	A	Birmingham City	1	2	
Sat	28	Feb	Div 1	H	Tottenham Hotspur	2	1	
Sat	7	Mar	Div 1	A	Manchester United	1	2	
Sat	14	Mar	Div 1	H	Blackpool	3	1	⊕
Sat	21	Mar	Div 1	A	Blackburn Rovers	1	2	
Fri	27	Mar	Div 1	A	Luton Town	1	0	
Sat	28	Mar	Div 1	H	Aston Villa	2	1	⊕
Mon	30	Mar	Div 1	H	Luton Town	3	1	
Sat	4	Apr	Div 1	A	West Ham United	2	3	⊕
Sat	11	Apr	Div 1	H	Nottingham Forest	1	3	⊕
Wed	15	Apr	Div 1	A	Portsmouth	3	2	
Sat	18	Apr	Div 1	A	Chelsea	1	3	
Sat	25	Apr	Div 1	H	Wolves	0	1	

EVERTON

1959-1960

Date			Competition	Venue	Opponents	Result		Goals
Sat	22	Aug	Div 1	H	Luton Town	2	2	⚽
Tue	25	Aug	Div 1	A	Burnley	2	5	
Sat	29	Aug	Div 1	A	Bolton Wanderers	1	2	⚽
Wed	2	Sep	Div 1	H	Burnley	1	2	
Sat	5	Sep	Div 1	H	Fulham	0	0	
Wed	16	Sep	Div 1	H	Blackburn Rovers	2	0	⚽⚽
Sat	19	Sep	Div 1	H	Sheffield Wednesday	2	1	
Mon	21	Sep	Div 1	A	Blackburn Rovers	1	3	
Sat	26	Sep	Div 1	A	Wolves	0	2	
Sat	10	Oct	Div 1	A	Leeds United	3	3	⚽⚽
Sat	17	Oct	Div 1	H	West Ham United	0	1	
Sat	24	Oct	Div 1	A	Chelsea	0	1	

LIVERPOOL

Sat	7	Nov	Div 2	H	Aston Villa	2	1	⚽⚽
Sat	14	Nov	Div 2	A	Lincoln City	2	4	⚽
Sat	21	Nov	Div 2	H	Leyton Orient	4	3	⚽
Sat	28	Nov	Div 2	A	Huddersfield Town	0	1	
Sat	5	Dec	Div 2	H	Ipswich Town	3	1	⚽
Sat	12	Dec	Div 2	A	Bristol Rovers	2	0	
Sat	19	Dec	Div 2	H	Cardiff City	0	4	
Sat	26	Dec	Div 2	A	Charlton Athletic	0	3	
Mon	28	Dec	Div 2	H	Charlton Athletic	2	0	
Sat	2	Jan	Div 2	A	Hull City	1	0	
Sat	9	Jan	FAC 3	H	Leyton Orient	2	1	
Sat	16	Jan	Div 2	H	Sheffield United	3	0	
Sat	23	Jan	Div 2	A	Middlesbrough	3	3	⚽
Sat	30	Jan	FAC 4	H	Manchester United	1	3	
Sat	13	Feb	Div 2	A	Plymouth Argyle	1	1	⚽
Sat	20	Feb	Div 2	H	Swansea Town	4	1	⚽⚽
Sat	27	Feb	Div 2	A	Brighton & Hove Albion	2	1	⚽⚽
Sat	5	Mar	Div 2	H	Stoke City	5	1	⚽
Sat	12	Mar	Div 2	A	Portsmouth	1	2	
Sat	19	Mar	Div 2	H	Huddersfield Town	2	2	⚽
Wed	30	Mar	Div 2	A	Aston Villa	4	4	⚽
Sat	2	Apr	Div 2	H	Lincoln City	1	3	
Wed	6	Apr	Div 2	H	Derby County	4	1	⚽
Sat	9	Apr	Div 2	A	Leyton Orient	0	2	
Sat	16	Apr	Div 2	H	Bristol Rovers	4	0	
Mon	18	Apr	Div 2	H	Rotherham United	3	0	⚽⚽
Tue	19	Apr	Div 2	A	Rotherham United	2	2	⚽
Sat	23	Apr	Div 2	A	Ipswich Town	1	0	⚽
Sat	30	Apr	Div 2	H	Sunderland	3	0	⚽

LIVERPOOL

1960-1961

Date			Competition	Venue	Opponents	Result		Goals
Sat	20	Aug	Div 2	H	Leeds United	2	0	⚽
Wed	24	Aug	Div 2	A	Southampton	1	4	
Sat	27	Aug	Div 2	A	Middlesbrough	1	1	
Sat	3	Sep	Div 2	H	Brighton & Hove Albion	2	0	
Wed	7	Sep	Div 2	H	Luton Town	2	2	⚽
Sat	10	Sep	Div 2	A	Ipswich Town	0	1	
Sat	24	Sep	Div 2	A	Leyton Orient	3	1	⚽
Sat	1	Oct	Div 2	H	Derby County	1	0	
Sat	8	Oct	Div 2	A	Lincoln City	2	1	
Sat	15	Oct	Div 2	H	Portsmouth	3	3	⚽⚽
Wed	19	Oct	LC 2	H	Luton Town	1	1	
Sat	22	Oct	Div 2	A	Huddersfield Town	4	2	⚽
Mon	24	Oct	LC 2 Rep	A	Luton Town	5	2	⚽
Sat	29	Oct	Div 2	H	Sunderland	1	1	
Sat	5	Nov	Div 2	A	Plymouth Argyle	4	0	⚽
Sat	12	Nov	Div 2	H	Norwich City	2	1	
Wed	16	Nov	LC 3	H	Southampton	1	2	
Sat	19	Nov	Div 2	A	Charlton Athletic	3	1	
Sat	26	Nov	Div 2	H	Sheffield United	4	2	⚽
Sat	10	Dec	Div 2	H	Swansea Town	4	0	⚽
Sat	17	Dec	Div 2	A	Leeds United	2	2	
Mon	26	Dec	Div 2	H	Rotherham United	2	1	
Tue	27	Dec	Div 2	A	Rotherham United	0	1	
Sat	31	Dec	Div 2	H	Middlesbrough	3	4	
Sat	7	Jan	FAC 3	H	Coventry City	3	2	
Sat	21	Jan	Div 2	H	Ipswich Town	1	1	
Sat	28	Jan	FAC 4	H	Sunderland	0	2	
Sat	4	Feb	Div 2	A	Scunthorpe United	3	2	
Sat	11	Feb	Div 2	H	Leyton Orient	5	0	⚽⚽⚽
Sat	18	Feb	Div 2	A	Derby County	4	1	⚽
Sat	25	Feb	Div 2	H	Lincoln City	2	0	
Fri	31	Mar	Div 2	H	Bristol Rovers	3	0	⚽
Sat	01	Apr	Div 2	A	Sheffield United	1	1	
Tue	04	Apr	Div 2	A	Bristol Rovers	3	4	
Sat	08	Apr	Div 2	H	Charlton Athletic	2	1	
Sat	15	Apr	Div 2	A	Norwich City	1	2	⚽
Sat	22	Apr	Div 2	H	Stoke City	3	0	⚽
Sat	29	Apr	Div 2	A	Sunderland	1	1	

DAVE HICKSON | THE CANNONBALL KID

BURY

1961-1962

Date			Competition	Venue	Opponents	Result		Goals
Sat	3	Feb	Div 2	A	Charlton Athletic	0	1	
Sat	10	Feb	Div 2	H	Liverpool	0	3	
Sat	24	Feb	Div 2	H	Luton Town	2	1	
Sat	3	Mar	Div 2	A	Newcastle United	2	1	
Sat	10	Mar	Div 2	H	Middlesbrough	2	1	
Tue	13	Mar	Div 2	H	Leyton Orient	0	1	
Sat	17	Mar	Div 2	A	Walsall	0	3	

TRANMERE ROVERS

1962-1963

Date			Competition	Venue	Opponents	Result		Goals
Sat	8	Sep	Div 4	H	Hartlepools United	6	1	
Mon	10	Sep	Div 4	H	Bradford City	1	1	⚽
Sat	15	Sep	Div 4	A	Darlington	3	2	⚽⚽
Mon	17	Sep	Div 4	H	Torquay United	1	1	⚽
Fri	21	Sep	Div 4	H	Southport	7	1	⚽⚽
Sat	29	Sep	Div 4	A	Aldershot	3	2	
Mon	1	Oct	Div 4	A	Mansfield Town	1	6	
Sat	6	Oct	Div 4	H	Doncaster Rovers	2	3	⚽
Sat	13	Oct	Div 4	A	Stockport County	2	2	⚽
Sat	20	Oct	Div 4	H	Gillingham	2	1	
Wed	24	Oct	Div 4	A	Bradford City	1	2	
Sat	27	Oct	Div 4	A	Crewe Alexandra	0	2	
Sat	3	Nov	FAC 1	A	Chester City	2	0	⚽
Sat	10	Nov	Div 4	A	York City	2	1	
Sat	24	Nov	FAC 2	A	Doncaster Rovers	4	1	⚽⚽
Sat	1	Dec	Div 4	H	Chesterfield	4	1	⚽⚽⚽
Sat	8	Dec	Div 4	A	Exeter City	1	2	
Sat	15	Dec	Div 4	H	Lincoln City	3	0	⚽
Sat	5	Jan	FAC 3	H	Chelsea	2	2	
Wed	30	Jan	FAC 3 Rep	A	Chelsea	1	3	⚽
Wed	27	Feb	Div 4	A	Oldham Athletic	1	1	
Sat	2	Mar	Div 4	H	Stockport County	3	1	⚽
Mon	4	Mar	Div 4	H	Brentford	1	2	⚽
Sat	9	Mar	Div 4	A	Gillingham	0	0	
Mon	11	Mar	Div 4	H	Oxford United	3	0	⚽⚽
Mon	25	Mar	Div 4	H	Darlington	3	1	
Sat	30	Mar	Div 4	H	Rochdale	3	2	⚽
Thu	4	Apr	Div 4	A	Oxford United	2	2	⚽
Sat	6	Apr	Div 4	A	Brentford	0	4	
Fri	12	Apr	Div 4	H	Newport County	0	0	
Sat	13	Apr	Div 4	H	York City	2	1	⚽
Sat	20	Apr	Div 4	A	Chesterfield	0	4	
Mon	22	Apr	Div 4	H	Mansfield Town	5	1	
Thu	25	Apr	Div 4	A	Doncaster Rovers	1	2	
Sat	27	Apr	Div 4	H	Exeter City	2	1	
Wed	1	May	Div 4	A	Torquay United	0	1	
Sat	4	May	Div 4	H	Aldershot	1	3	

DAVE HICKSON | THE CANNONBALL KID

TRANMERE ROVERS

1963-1964

Date			Competition	Venue	Opponents	Result		Goals
Sat	24	Aug	Div 4	A	Torquay United	1	1	
Mon	26	Aug	Div 4	H	York City	1	0	
Fri	30	Aug	Div 4	H	Carlisle United	6	1	⚽
Wed	4	Sep	LC 1	H	Stockport County	2	0	
Sat	7	Sep	Div 4	A	Aldershot	4	5	⚽
Mon	9	Sep	Div 4	A	York City	2	1	
Fri	13	Sep	Div 4	H	Bradford City	0	1	
Mon	16	Sep	Div 4	A	Halifax Town	0	2	
Sat	21	Sep	Div 4	A	Lincoln City	1	0	
Wed	25	Sep	LC 2	H	Southampton	2	0	
Fri	27	Sep	Div 4	D	Gillingham	0	0	
Mon	30	Sep	Div 4	H	Halifax Town	2	2	
Sat	5	Oct	Div 4	A	Southport	0	2	
Wed	16	Oct	LC 3	H	Leicester City	1	2	
Fri	18	Oct	Div 4	H	Oxford United	1	3	

<u>DAVID HICKSON.</u>

This is the story of Dave Hickson from Ellesmere Port,
Where many famous footballers were taught.
In 1946 he joined the Everton junior school,
And soon showed the opposition he was no fool.
As a goalscorer he began to make his mark,
And that is how he began his career at Goodison Park.
Then after a two year wait,
He turned professional in 1948.
Into the reserves he soon played his way,
And a big improvement was shown in his play.
Against Sheffield Reserves he scored five of Everton's eight,
And that was when Everton never scored at that rate.
He made his league debut on the 1st of September,
A day I am sure we will always remember,
For that was Evertons first win away,
And Dave played his part in the victory that day.
Then after three games into the reserves he went,
And many letters of criticism to Cliff Britton were sent.
But Cliff wanted to impress on him that getting to the top is tough,
So Dave decided to cool down and not be so rough.
Then October the 27th he made his return,
And showed that he had been willing to learn,
His play showed a big improvement all round,
And we began to relize Everton a grand Centre-Forward had found.
He began to get goals like Centre-Forwards should,
And he showed how easily he could adapt himself in the mud.
He stayed in the first team till March the 22nd then he lost his
                                          place,
And into the reserves he went lesser teams to face,
Into his place stepped Gwyn our little Welsh lad,
Because Cliff wanted to give him a chance even though Dave's play
                                          hadn't been bad.
True in the last few games he hadn't been at his brilliant best,
But even so Dave to the opposition had still proved a pest.
The first team lost and they missed Dave in the attack,
Because although Gwyn's football was good in Dave's thrust he did
                                          lack.
Dave came back the following week to lead the Blues,
And to the end of the season only two games they did lose.
He has injected into the forwards the bite they always did lack,
To transform them from an ordinary to a brilliant attack.
He can shoot and move at a very fast speed,
And he never forgets his other forwards to feed.
It is a wonderful sight to watch Dave head,
But by his robust play many Centre-Halves see red.
But when he plays clean it is a wonderful sight,
Much better than when he gets rough and decides to fight.
I hope Dave will soon get his International Cap,
And like Joe Mercer put his town on the map.
Off the field he is a nice quiet decent sort,
Is our Dave Hickson from Ellesmere Port.

This poem was found among Dave's belongings shortly after he passed away. Its author remains unknown.

Also by deCoubertin Books

Binman Chronicles by Neville Southall.

ISBN: 9780956431387. £18.99

Considered among the greatest goalkeepers of all time and one of English football's defining figures over a career that spanned more than two decades, Neville Southall has for the first time decided to tell his extraordinary life story. Uncompromising, unorthodox and often unkempt, Southall's career followed an incredible trajectory: from football-mad binman, to the greatest goalkeeper in the world in the space of a few years. Southall's amazing story is the ultimate antidote to the dull stereotype of the modern footballer.

Everton Encyclopedia by James Corbett.

ISBN: 978-0956431349. £35.00

In this mammoth landmark book, author James Corbett has chronicled the individuals and incidents that made Everton into the great institution that we know today. With entries on every man to pull on an Everton shirt, including more than 450 full biographical entries, some 350,000 words and utilising new and original research from the recently opened Everton Collection, Corbett's book crosses new boundaries in the study of Evertonia. Lavishly illustrated and printed in full colour throughout this is a book that will be passed down through generations of Evertonians.

Harry Catterick: The Untold Story of a Football great by Rob Sawyer.

978-1909245181. £18.99

As the manager of Sheffield Wednesday and Everton, Harry Catterick amassed more top flight points in the 1960s than all his rivals, finishing outside the top six on only one occasion. Yet, unfairly, he stands in the shadows of contemporaries such as Bill Shankly, Don Revie and Brian Clough in the public consciousness. Following extensive research, including being given unique access to the Catterick family's documents and photographs, Rob Sawyer has recounted the life of this football great for the very first time.

Love Affairs and Marriage: My Life in Football by Howard Kendall.

ISBN: 978-1909245068. £20.00

Howard Kendall is one of the greats of English football management and among the defining figures in the history of Everton Football Club. A schoolboy prodigy footballer, he first joined the club from Preston in 1967, forming one of the most distinguished midfield partnerships ever witnessed in the English game. He won the League Championship in 1970 and later captained the club. He returned to Goodison as manager in 1981, reviving Everton for the most successful period in their history. Now he lifts the lid on a 30-year career that established his reputation.

Everton: The School of Science by James Corbett.

9780956431332. £9.99.

In his highly acclaimed history of one of the country's most distinguished teams, James Corbett traces the fortunes of Everton Football Club from their humble origins as a church team to the David Moyes era. From Fred Geary to Alex Young and Dixie Dean through to such modern icons as Mikel Arteta and Tim Cahill, Everton: The School of Science takes in the stories of all the men who make the club great. Everton: The School of Science is the definitive history of one of English football's aristocrats; an engrossing and graphic account of the inside stories, glories and shattered dreams of 'The People's Club'.